CÆSURA: ESSAYS

Gary McDowell

CÆSURA: ESSAYS

OTIS BOOKS | SEISMICITY EDITIONS
The Graduate Writing Program
Otis College of Art and Design
LOS ANGELES O 2017

Book design and typesetting: George Dino Fekaris

ISBN-13: 978-0-9860836-4-8

OTIS BOOKS | SEISMICITY EDITIONS
The Graduate Writing Program
Otis College of Art and Design
9045 Lincoln Boulevard
Los Angeles, CA 90045

http://www.otis.edu/graduate-writing/otis-books
seismicity@otis.edu

While I tried to remember the last time I had cried,
I cried.

— GARY YOUNG

ACKNOWLEDGMENTS

Grateful acknowledgment is made to the following journals where the corresponding essays first appeared, though some in different forms:

Bellingham Review: "Bricks by Type"
DIAGRAM: "On Whining"
Eleven Eleven: "*What Is Found There*: On Beauty"
The Fourth River: "Postlude on Darkness" as "Interlude on Darkness"
Green Mountains Review (as winner of the 2014 Neil Shepard Prize in Creative Nonfiction): "An Eye that Never Closes in Sleep: A Nightbook"
Gulf Coast: "The Emptying that Fills"
Iron Horse Literary Review: "Your Body Moves You Though You Wish It Wouldn't"
The Laurel Review: "...the inability to isolate a sensation..."
The Massachusetts Review: "How to Cope with Risk"
NANO*fiction*: "Confession"
Quarter After Eight: "Hiatus: A Memoir in Cæsura"
Prairie Schooner (as runner-up in the 2013 Creative Nonfiction Prize): "There Are Manuals for Those"
SLAB: "It's Just a Bear, Asshole"
The Southern Review: "Rhythm is Originally the Rhythm of the Feet"
The Turnip Truck(s): "Another Animal: Variations on a Scene, and a Coda"

*

Thank you Guy Bennett and the Otis Books | Seismicity Editions crew for believing in this book and for taking a chance on it. To my students and colleagues at Belmont University, you are all constant beacons of support and encouragement: thank you. To the folks who read early versions of these essays and persuaded me to keep going, you are the best: Susan Finch, Traci Brimhall, and Alex Lemon. And as always, for the time to write and the love to write well, thank you Mandy, Auden, and Jorie. Everything is always for you.

TABLE OF CONTENTS

LYRICISM OF THE FACT: AN ARCHIVE

Archive, *noun*: 3) any extensive record or collection of data. Synonymns: annals, chronicles, clippings, documents, excerpts, extracts, files, papers, registers, rolls, scrolls, writings.

When using this template, the following steps are recommended:

Replace all text enclosed in angle brackets with the correct field document values.

Modify boilerplate text as appropriate for the specific project.

The United States has never lost a war in which mules were used.

Eclipses exist because the moon is 400 times smaller than the sun but also 400 times closer to the Earth.

Geometry is *an event of interest.*

Possible topic headings for an historical archive:

Events of Interest

Operational Informational Details

Intelligence Gathering

Research Value

Administrative Value
Legal Value
Appraisal
Accessioning

A team of medical experts in Virginia contends you're more likely to catch the common cold virus by shaking hands than by kissing.

The German language contains thirty words that refer to the act of kissing, including one, *Nachkuss*, for all the kisses that haven't yet been named.

Amorous Canadian porcupines kiss one another on the lips

THE EMPTYING THAT FILLS

The mind is hurried out of itself, by a crowd of great and confused images; which affect because they are crowded and confused. For separate them, and you lose much of the greatness, and join them, and you infallibly lose the clearness.

— EDMUND BURKE

I can envision coming back as something other than, larger or smaller or altogether shifted, off-compass like a coastline, a vulture, a boy running ahead of his father in the forest. As raindrops. The parallel lines of their fall and the uniformity of their sound and their wetness, yes. I'd like to fear the falling, or be feared for falling, or be myself what is feared most: inexhaustible, as clouds, as moisture. Such is/as faith. Such is responsibility and believing in something untenuous, animal-driven, needed.

My son and I are taking an early fall hike through Long Hunter State Park just outside Nashville. We walk the two-mile loop around Couchville Lake, weave the cone-shaped fishing waters, watch for deer and turkey and kids hoping for bluegill, listen to wind through the treetops and crows or ravens and the last of the cicadas zinging. All the noises, except a distant twig cracking underfoot, we cannot spy, come from above our heads.

Maybe I could come back as a tree: blackgum, pignut, hophornbeam, the varieties we see outlined on the State Park sponsored plaques posted every quarter-mile along the path. Trees like poetry, like fatherhood – we speak in cataracts and pristine stillness while the world sleeps and while the world watches – augment and negotiate segmentivities: branches hang low over the walking path, their hatchet-shadows and their dancing, partition, apparition, whatever ghost-lights through the canopy. We are here, on the ground and moving, and they are there, from the ground and still, except to shift at the weather.

Elias Canetti, in his *Crowds and Power*, makes of the forest a symbol, tells us that *the forest is the first image of awe*. My son, running ahead of me on the trail now, shrinks into distance, but he is still level, still plained, capable of moving further-away or closer-to but incapable of moving up or overhead. *Man stands upright like a tree and he inserts himself amongst the other trees. But they are taller than he is and he has to look up at them. No other natural phenomenon of his surroundings is invariably above him and, at the same time, so near and so multiple in its formations as the concourse of trees.* I follow him, wind around a corner or two, find him again, his arms twirling, his head bouncing above and then below and then above the horizon created by the rise and dip of the trail. Every few paces he stops to look up, so I slow to let him. *Looking up at trees becomes looking up in general. The forest is a preparation for the feeling of being in church, the standing before God among pillars and columns.*

Part of me thinks I know him better now having watched him look up, search without knowing for what he searches. I want to know him better *now, here, forever*, or at least *before*. But I can't answer *before-what?* Canetti tells us, *tree-tops are attainable.* Frost: *He is all pine and I am all apple orchard.* Maybe that's enough? He's mine like an apple is the tree's? He's mine like a needle is the pine tree's? He's neither mine nor his own? My fear: I'll never be sated of him before this or that, or I'll never be able to *appreciate* (to gain in meaning or value) his closeness: he'll always want to run ahead of me far enough so that all I'll be able to see is his head tilting, his eyes locking onto something above.

*

Tam Mai shows me a picture of his most recent painting. A waterfall, its white-crush, violent and moving, an inventory of fear or beauty, or a scar askew. The water folds into a black pool, the rocks jutted, the shrubbery around the scene both stoic and spined. Vietnam. *My home country*, he always tells me, as though *Vietnam* crossing his lips would make it more real – or less real.

He empties the trash in my office, tells me, *scroll next one*. The same waterfall but this time there are shadows in the water and the water darkens at the base of the falls. A face or two ovals and a crescent, hair or wispy branches and leaves, and then, opalescent and dissoluted, another face, this one with longer hair and no pupils, something of a ghost, an apparition, a disembodied grass-sky-tree, *the-emptying-that-fills*, an ancestor and what it feels like to believe.

He tells me, the waterfall is the mother. The pool is the father. Gravity is the pressure to obey. *Only mother kisses child. Only mother the child knows for sure. Father? Could be. Could be not.* The threat of drowning permeates the culture, and the children that play along the skirt of the waterfall flirt with salvation, encourage the spirit of the not-father to push them over the edge into the pool *too deep for children to touch*. Rain floods the jungle surrounding the fall every spring. Tam: *Trouble everywhere. Nights spent under water. Feet blister from the wet. How to escape wasn't an idea.*

The drowned speak in unison, it is said. In the night they make noises – at dawn the night never existed. What they fear isn't the dark water but that they aren't conscious fully when the light seeps back in.

*

To better appreciate *practice*, maybe *reprieve*, or *to study*, let's take a quick tour with our resident arborist.

The blackgum to our left has a straight trunk though the branches extend outward at right angles. The bark, furrowed with age. The twigs, when we reach to snap them, break easily to reveal the pith: chambers of greenish partitions. Little cells, not jails or rooms, but mitochondrial engines, airy pockets defined.

The leaves: elliptical, obovate, lustrous and entire. We roll them between our fingers, crush the purple-red to crumbs, make a cocoa-colored mess in our palms. Look! The flowers have fruited on a lower branch, one outside our initial field of vision: a black-blue, ovoid fruit. Our field guide tells us that it has a thin, oily, bitter-to-sour taste. We don't dare, though we should. Fleshy drupe – one to three from each flower cluster. The fruit's stone, more or less ridged. October. Early October. The click of consonants on the roofs of our mouths, a stone rolled click-clack, click-clack like a mint against our teeth.

We run our hands along the blackgum's trunk, peel off a small piece or two of bark. Pale yellow, sapwood. White even, if the light. *Not durable in contact with the soil.* But who's to say what's *stable*, what's *which*? Further we reach. I put my son on my shoulders, ask him to run a leaf through his fingers, tell me what he feels. *Rusty feathers*, he says. I didn't know he knew those words in combination. Our guide tells us, *wedge-shaped with margin slightly thickened, acute or acuminate. They come out of the bud conduplicate. Feather-veined, midrib and primary veins prominent beneath. Petioles one-quarter to one-half an inch long, slender or stout, terete or margined, often red.* Encyclopedic: the music of nature's Nature.

Here is where science ends and poetry begins. Or maybe they're one and the same always: *Moby Dick. Nature. Leaves of Grass.* We touch the tree because it's on the path, because we can't understand it better without holding a part of it in our hands. When my son's in trouble, I grab his arm, pull him close to me, watch his eyes and reprimand slowly. He understands he should shift his eyes from mine, should do everything to squirm away, and he will try. But something holds him close. The gravitas of fathers-sons, the noise of close-watching, of observation, of knowing something's intrinsic importance before its utterance.

Our arborist keeps talking. Here our arborist pauses, considers his next explanation. *Definitionally speaking, I don't mean to lose you here, but this* – A dismissive wave of his hand. *Anyway, I will carry on then. You can undoubtedly follow.* The language is never the problem. The delivery, however. The tone, mood. Anatomy of intent, to stray ourselves from apathy.

I put my son back on the ground. He walks ahead, sees a turkey, gobbles at it and laughs. The turkey, confused, struts, complicates the sexual obliviousness of the season.

The pignut, shagwork, mockernut. *A hickory, you see.* Hickories are monoecious, hermaphroditic, and their bole is often forked. A tongue split two ways, a tree that knows multiple voices, that always faces light and dark simultaneously. The staminate catkins – wind-pollinated flowering spikes – of pignut hickory develop from *axils of leaves of the previous season or from inner scales of the terminal buds at the base of the current growth.* Or exactly like Darwin suggested: survival.

Husks of pignut hickory split only to the middle or slightly beyond and generally cling to the nut, which is unribbed, with a thick shell. My son wanders over the next ridge in the trail. I call him back. Protection then, in the shadow: think of the otherwise danger. The dream surrendered. The arborist caresses an unsplit husk, pushes it to his lips, the wax of what's left, practices the wind, says, *shhhhhhh* and *listen*.

He tells of other trees, ones hard-wooded, ones delicious in the shade, in moonlight, under the blue-black nevertheless known or unknown sky. *I'm not one to say,* last but not least, *but, last but not least: the Ostrya, the hophornbeam.* The arborist mimics us reaching out to touch, so we do. Scaly, rough bark. Alternate and double-toothed birch-like leaves, flowerless until spring when their fruit is a *small nut fully enclosed in a bladder-like involucre.*

The name Ostrya is derived from the Greek word "ostrua," "bone-like," referring to the very hard wood. Regarded as a weed tree by some foresters, this hard and stable wood was historically used to fashion plane soles. My son, weaving down the path, his arms jutted out parallel to the ground as wings, dips left and right, curving, urging the engine noise from deep in his throat.

*

"Moonlight hanging or dropping on treetops like blue cobweb. Also the upper sides of little grotted waves turned to the sky have soft pale-coloured cobwebs on them, the under sides green."

Gerard Manley Hopkins, *An Early Diary*, "April (?), 1864"

*

"You have to get obsessed, stay obsessed, and keep passing open windows."

John Irving, *The Hotel New Hampshire*

In June of 1992 I found a box in the parking lot of the Cary Area Public Library. Among the things I threw out: two five-pound dumbbells, a jump rope, an empty box of Rogaine, some old Twizzlers, and a stick of deodorant. What I kept: four issues of *High Society*, two issues of *Hustler*, a long-distance calling card, and a beat-up pair of weightlifting gloves. And for that entire summer, when I wasn't lost in an issue of one of those magazines, I mowed the lawn wearing the sweat-stained weightlifting gloves. They made the job less job-like and more manly. I sweat, I gripped that sonuvabitch mower as tightly as I could, Metallica's *And Justice for All* on Side A and Weird Al's *Even Worse* on Side B, the Walkman cranked as high as it would go.

*

"It may be regarded as a projection, a climax, a badge of strength, power or vigour, a tapering body, a spiral, a wavy object, a bow, a vessel to hold withal or to drink from, a smooth hard material not brittle, stony, metallic or wooden, something sprouting up, something to thrust or push with, a sign of honour or pride, an instrument of music, etc."

Gerard Manley Hopkins, *An Early Diary*, "September 24, 1863"

*

I wish I could paint you a picture of the rock. It was all colors at once, especially purple and silver and brown and gray and light and moon and clouds (backlit, naturally) and chrome, chipped primer maybe. And when the hundreds (or thousands) of box elder bugs crowded onto it, black and orange and black and orange like the blues and whites of "The Great Wave Off Kanagawa," frothing and foaming and yet static: *Pictures of the Floating World.* I mowed around it, thinking each time that the box elder bugs would scatter, but they never moved or even flinched. I tried to aim the grass thrown from the mower away from them. Their peace became important to my peace. Even youth perceives quiet, appreciates the calm of a not-decision, of being at another's whim.

They gathered on the rock to judge its worthiness as a place to overwinter, at least that's what I learned later at the public library. The silver maple they called home all spring and early summer wouldn't do for the cold months. *Otherwise known as a zug or a maple bug or a stink bug.* They sought a warm, dry place for winter, thought the rock, warm because of the summer sun, would be that shelter, and so they clamored to it, laid claim to it, covered its surface in hopes that it would warm them from the coming cold.

*

Q: Why are poets so fascinated with autumn?

A: Because squirrels bury nuts—I've always wondered, how do they find them later? Surely they could find *a* buried acorn, but how do they find the ones they themselves buried? Maybe, and I'm imagining that squirrels have an olfactory ability akin to moles, they smell their way through the vast parkgrounds and forests until they twitch upon the scent of their own saliva—the hormones, the bacteria, the after-food-and-gender-and-blood—their shit, their urine, some marker or another that sets their acorns apart. Or maybe it doesn't matter. Maybe a nut is a nut and against the brute reality of winter starvation they simply choose survival over the pettiness of good manners.

It gets darker earlier in autumn: more time to research questions like this, and so we, poets, admire the autumnal shift in light, the candor, the tilt, the buoyant full-colored grace of old and new, the receding and rising-dropping of one orb for another.

For me it was this: "Their sons grow suicidally beautiful / At the beginning of October, / And gallop terribly against each other's bodies." For me it was Wright's other poem where at the end of summer, "in a field of sunlight between two pines," as the butterfly slows down, the hammock swings softly, and the poet whispers, "I have wasted my life." Maybe James Wright is autumn like Plath is winter like Roethke is summer like Whitman is spring. There's the vacating–the already left–feeling of autumn. It's the coming of cold that makes us cold, and.... Let me start over. In the morning just before sunrise, there's a color at the eastern edge of the land-sky slope. It's *roseate. Coral. Flush*, with the un-light of the sun and the blush of the early fog. Here, this bloom, this scallop–its efflorescence: a pity more are dreaming through its bursting–disentangles the night from its corollary, night from what should be unnamable: harvest, consequence, yielding.

My mom swaddled me too tightly as a baby, and so now I run hot. I hate being warm. I'm a poet, but for a long time I thought it was my body that was fucked up.

*

I just read on cnn.com today that the Mbendjele Yaka of northern Congo believe Europe is the afterlife. Forest-living hunter-gatherers considered the first inhabitants of their region, the author writes that they avoid contact with the *exterior world* to maintain autonomy. They believe that all Europeans are spirits and hope that someday they'll be born again as Europeans.

I have a friend who thinks that eventually mainland California will break-off, *disengage*, he says, as if the land will stop its conversation, turn its back on implicit metaphor and symbolic he-said-she-said, of the continental US and cause a tsunami that will engulf, flood, *ocean-palette* Hawaii. Locusts. Earthquakes. Tornadoes. Superstorms, with names. To come back as a natural disaster, god-like, ravaging, migrating. Flock, how birds sense, and leap or lift or *plume*, a coming quake or wave, something disruptive—a warning we're likely to ignore. To come back as that flock, the cosmic, the consciousness, the worldly Over: if the land leaves the land that holds it and depresses, pushes the stars to the peripheral, upends what stands, what floats, what can *overcome*, cup your hand to your ear and listen for the flutter of feathers and hollow bones taking to the sky. Go, then, the opposite direction.

*

Paul Radin, *The Winnebago Tribe*, 1923, as told by Thunder Cloud, a Winnebago shaman:

I was taken to the place where the sun sets. ... While at that place, I thought I would come back to earth again, and the old man with whom I was staying said to me, "My son, did you not speak about wanting to go to the earth again?" I had, as a matter of fact, only thought of it, yet he knew what I wanted. Then he said to me, "You can go, but you must ask the chief first." Then I went and told the chief of the village of my desire, and he said to me, "You may go and obtain your revenge upon the people who killed your relatives and you." Then I was brought down to earth. ... There I lived until I died of old age.... As I was lying [in my grave], someone said to me, "Come, let us go away." So then we went toward the setting of the sun. There we came to a village where we met all the dead....

From that place I came to this earth again for the third time, and here I am.

*

What I don't realize is that I can't hide that, loyal or not, we are all doomed. To one go-round, one set of beats, breaths, calibrations. Pop songs often get everything wrong, but sometimes they get it right:

I hope I die before I get old. And.

I ain't as good as I once was. And.

For it's hard, you will find, to be narrow of mind. Exactly.

Are we a peace-loving people despite the evidence? And how can a thing that's evident itself also be evidence? I heard a story on the radio about a man who bet his wife his Chicago Bears would beat her Green Bay Packers. The winner would get to taze the loser for three seconds. In public. On the street. The Bears won. Both drunk, they stumbled outside the bar in Smalltown, Wisconsin, and he touched the electric fire to her ass, burned her through the denim as spittle spilled through her lips, as her eyes rolled, as *eyewitness accounts.* She then called the police, had him arrested for "intent to harm with an electronic weapon." Patience. He had none. Had he known better the *scope,* the ramifications, the dimensions, for one thing, of *trust me, it'll only hurt a little, for a second,* maybe he'd have gloated instead. I can see him grabbing his rib cage as he belly-laughs, his wife crumbled on the ground, smoke rising from her burnt jeans, and then the sound of sirens later, once she *regained,* once she sobered, the crowd by now dispersed.

The seed of an eastern wahoo, a Carolina buckthorn, can travel from the Outer Banks to the Tennessee woods in the belly of a warbler. To come back displaced. To come back rendered in love with soil redder, more clay-like: *the human body as distinguished from the spirit.* To be born through deposit, through shit, to loosen control, root where dropped, and take time, multiple seasons, to sprout, if warmth and wet and will combine, if a squirrel or shrew doesn't nip your first green bud, your first shoot shot through the soil. *I shall die, but / that is all that I shall do for Death.*

Somehow, I believe in the coming-back, and I owe this credence to some faith I don't understand. To come back as a witness, to come back as another kind of patience, the way trees grow, ringed and known only afterward, after the years are counted aloud.

HOW TO COPE WITH RISK

> *"I will do anything to avoid boredom.*
> *It is the task of a lifetime."*
> — ANNE CARSON, *Short Talks*

A lot of people say they have faith, which I take to mean they have fewer questions. Maybe that's backwards? Having questions, after all, is a prerequisite for having answers.

*

"We think we've figured it out. Your DUA was off."

After a few seconds of silence, the response from Apollo 12 was, "What is a DUA?"

"Digital Uplink Assembly," replied Houston.

*

An antapology is a reply to an apology, saying "It's all good" after someone in line apologizes for elbowing you in the ribs.

"I'm sorry I didn't explain that better."

"It's okay. I understand."

*

Being at home. In a place. Belief in any one thing over another feels like that; enveloping, a ceasing of *absence*.

Ubiety: thereness; being in a place. The -ness of believing and being—an idea spawns questions but a list spawns hints, answers, something like a jumping bean: alive, mysterious, altogether miraculous until you receive the explanation.

Then it's *just* nature.

*

In Radiohead's "Just," Thom Yorke sings: "Can't get the stink off / He's been hanging around for days / Comes like a comet / Suckered you but not your friends / One day he'll get to you / And teach you how to be a holy cow." I have to believe that this isn't a metaphor.

*

Defining a *space* is even harder than being in one. Like *storage*, or parental instinct, or *thou*, 0.0001 inches. It's *redefinition* that matters most—or at all. It's what you don't know, what you don't worry about. A privacy. *Space*. I haven't always lived here, but I find myself increasingly in the *Word Treasury*, the dictionary, the language inside the language inside my head.

My daughter is learning consequence: *No, don't touch that, honey*. And then she touches it anyway. The space where I discipline, where she imagines no one can see her—she acts, and though I stare at her, she's convinced that if she moves smoothly and slowly enough, she'll be invisible.

*

I don't know how else to say much of this except to talk around it. It's the possibility of stumbling that I chase. A slip: into something more comfortable. Or less.

I had a friend who ended up in the ER with a BAC of 0.45%. I asked him *why*. He said, *I didn't even know. I thought I was fine. It happened so fast.* I asked him *how*. He said, *a few beers, a bottle of this, a bottle of that*, and laughed.

*

We're still friends. But the past tense—*I had a friend*—invites you better into this *space. I ran a marathon* is easier to document than *I'm running a marathon.*

The advantage of nostalgia.

*

What I'm looking for is akin to *understanding,* but it's less precise than that, likely an as-of-yet-unnamed quality. A *mux,* which according to TIME is a blend of mix and flux, a lot of things going through (or over and around) one's head. Always the prepositional.

*

I know intuitively that someday I'll no longer be this body, but what then *becomes*? Like birds that migrate across seasons, across the equator, only to summer in winter and summer in summer, maybe we don't die so much as we transition. This is nothing new. *Nothing* is nothing new.

Christian Wiman writes that you can't really know religion,

belief, *anything from nothing*, from the outside because from there it remains "mere information, so long as your soul is not at risk."

*

We role-play, and I'm a cosmically ubiquitous fly-on-the-wall.

*

Opening and repetition. *I had a friend.* At the Art Institute of Chicago in the spring of 2008, I couldn't look away from a Georgia O'Keefe painting—the title escapes me, and a simple Google Image search turns up the visual but no information. An egg, partially hollowed near the top as though soft-boiled and scooped for breakfast, hued unnaturally brown—perhaps *organic* ahead of its time?—rests on white miniature mountains, or teeth, something deciduous and peaked, the whole resting on tan bedsheets, rumpled and ruffled as if the egg, having been eaten, caressed, cared *for*, is now tired and must sleep amongst the teeth that chewed it.

*

I just found an old Moleskin labeled "Spring/Summer 2008." Tucked into the pocket at the back I find a folded piece of loose-leaf paper with the following notes scribbled:

"Red and Pink Rocks and Teeth," 1938, O'Keefe, oil on canvas.

Random thought, first thought, best thought:

egged driftwood, molars –
oh, and the egg came first,
surely we know that now.
perception and enamel: how often
I've forgotten my wife's pregnant
belly, the hard surface of life,
the fight under the skin. this
is hollow, this ovum, this oval,

*

Telepathy. Connective tissue. I write two things, you conjure the third, the unspoken, the *meant*, or meat or ticket or *how often I've forgotten*–. The intensity of the space – the dreamy-space – before sleep, after waking. The in-between we chase, to be awake to the world while asleep.

*

Being observant. Give in to the impulse to chronicle, to be aware of *passing*, of calm and noise and what emerges – the ground squirrel from his hole while I mowed the lawn, my momentary fear that the blades would tear into him, though surely he's faster than sound.

Am I remembering correctly that Heidegger writes about the *falling-dream* being the *night-view* of daytime worries? Or maybe that was a TV psychologist.

*

Life is too short for memoir: push the beds together to make a fort.

*

Before there was the speed of light, there wasn't.

So, what was constant? How was anything measured with certainty? 186,000 mi/sec. We can't see it, can only *observe* it, in theory, in space, through time.

Preposition is constant; there wasn't, there is, above and below. An apple doesn't fall from a tree; gravity reacts against it. Or something like that.

*

My stepdad, Jim, in the summer of 1988, dug dozens of footings in our backyard. Three decks – from the house, then down a level, then down another level to the edging of the above-ground pool – three levels, three days of post hole digging, laser-sighted triangulations and measurements.

We turned on the porch lights at dusk, but day waned until soon June bugs scattered to the bulbs, a flurry of hard wings against the lightboxes. Bruised wings clacking, still trying. But what? Where did they want to go? "Almost done," he'd say, and then start clamshelling another 40" hole – that deep to protect, to build *foundation*, to stand up to the freeze in winter.

I remember, late one night, standing on the roof of the garage looking over all of the holes. Jim leaned against the house, remembering *measure twice, dig once*, and I swear I saw, in the depths of the holes, the reflection of each fleck of star in the night sky, wholly contained, and constant.

This is faith.

*

All of this befuddlement and incantatory trickery – *nothing, anything, something, becomes* – life and death, *space* and idea: neither, both, and all of the *above*.

Coping comes with the present.

WHAT IS FOUND THERE: ON BEAUTY

I have to say to you / and you alone / but it must wait /
while I drink in / the joy of your approach...
— WILLIAM CARLOS WILLIAMS,
from "Asphodel, That Greeny Flower"

I was a boy. It was an effort to not feed the birds, their mottled gray
dew-dropped and smooth like history in love with bread – those
who declare themselves gods and those who believe it. Done
right, want is simply a question unanswerable. Done right, need
is want disguised as a mouthful of air. And beauty, or the pursuit
of its aftermath – joy – is only for the hungry.

*

Don't feed the birds. The ubiquity of that sign. At zoos. At parks.
At pet stores. But the zoo, the one I remember most. The flamingos like dancers, but paused, mid-leap, the knee-bend hy-
perbolic, or maybe just hyper-extended. But *still.* Admit it, you've
tried it – in yoga it's called, of course, The Flamingo Pose – upon
seeing one at the zoo until you toppled, grabbed the guardrail,
looked around, and *no, no one saw you* – the other leg tucked beneath the body. Recent research indicates that standing on one
leg allows the flamingo to conserve more body heat, given that
they spend a significant amount of time wading in cool water.

Less a dance, more a survival.

But Baryshnikov: *I cannot stand authority. And I am restless. Always restless.*

Flamingos stomp their webbed feet in the mud to stir up food from the bottom. Less a dance, more a survival.

A wading bird in the genus Phoenicopterus, from the Greek, meaning *purple wing*. Adults range from light pink to bright red. The amount of aqueous bacteria and beta-Carotene obtained from their food supply dictates their shading. Captive flamingos turn a pale pink as they are not fed beta-Carotene at levels comparable to the wild.

Flamingos filter-feed on brine shrimp and blue-green algae. Their beaks are specially adapted to separate mud and silt from the food they eat, and are uniquely used upside-down. *Comparable to the wild*: I'm a little ashamed that that phrase doesn't bother me more.

*

The first flamingo hatched in a zoo was a Chilean Flamingo at Zoo Basel in Switzerland in 1958. Since then, over 389 flamingos have grown up in Basel and been distributed to other zoos around the globe.

*

I'm in college. I'm drinking a Miller Lite at the bar: hubcaps as wall décor and framed centerfolds where dartboards might usually hang.

I think: I've heard coyotes in packs but only ever seen one at a time. Where do they go in the deep dusk?

And then she comes back to the bar.

I think: Pack animals sleep in shifts and the tallest building in the world will never again be American.

Somehow facts never disappoint, as if the dumbbells in the corner of the bar's bathroom are there not to prop the door during Happy Hour but rather to curl or press while waiting in line for the urinal.

She leans over, her drunk rasp tickles my ear: *I think that guy's looking at me.* I don't have it in me to tell her that he's looking at Miss October 1992 in the frame behind her, but I also don't know which of us is lying.

*

I was a boy dreaming I was a boy dreaming as I cut the grass. I didn't see it, couldn't have, through the lushness, the green, the width of the mower deck – sweat in my eyes. The blade scooped the toad from the wet grass, spit it from the chute against the beige siding of the house. Redyellow, blueorange, one leg, one eye, the interior of the exterior, vice versa. What I'd seen before, in dissection or in textbooks – this is necessary: it's history in procession. In the Bible, a snake. In the Bible, a stutterer – and in the yard a toad, a blossom unlocked from the dirt: what if I greet you now asleep, what if I bury you in a field.

*

In Margret and H.A. Rey's *Curious George Feeds the Animals*, we see, on the last page, a warning: *Don't Feed the Animals!* But of course – because *This is George. George was a good little monkey and always very curious* – George feeds the animals, but only during the course of his search for the missing parrot from the zoo's new rain forest exhibit. George learned his behavior: the seals are fed by a zookeeper, so George feeds – using the peanuts purchased by The Man with the Yellow Hat (a subversive Bond villain? some kind of 19-century explorer? I'm still unsure and think perhaps he's a spy from another century) – the crocodiles, the koalas, the elephants, the baby kangaroo. An ostrich. A hippopotamus. Oh! Giraffes! *But as soon as he held out his hand [to the giraffes], a zookeeper came running. The zookeeper looked angry. Was he angry with George?* There's something so innocent here, something mysterious. We know anger, we know disappointment, we know discipline, and we wish to slip away from all of them, simultaneously. *Don't Feed the Animals!* Of course, we know this, but George is a curious monkey. Serendipitously, George finds the lost parrot when it swoops down to the bench where he sits to snack on a peanut. The zookeeper finds him there, with the parrot, and now George, our antagonist, is our protagonist. A perfect scenario. A little coincidence never hurt anyone. *George had an idea.* He so often does.

*

In America: Flamingos, bright pink ones, made of plastic, are anchored in front yards, side yards, backyards. A symbol of... wait, what the hell do they symbolize? An example of kitsch? A prank? *Fill the neighbor's yard with an entire flock!* But isn't toilet paper cheaper? And faster? And what about eggs? Or the steaming brown paper bag? God knows there's no shortage of dog shit on suburbia's lawns.

Little known fact: the original Pink Flamingo – designed by Don Featherstone in 1957 for Union Products – was sold only in pairs. How romantic. One stands upright, one stands with its head bent low. Eating? Drinking? *Feeding?*

In 1979, students at the University of Wisconsin, Madison covered the quad with 1,008 Featherstone originals. Some 27 years later, November 1, 2006 officially, production of the ubiquitous kitsch stopped.

In Ancient Egypt, the flamingo was considered a living representation of the god Ra.

In Ancient Rome, the flamingo's tongue was considered a delicacy.

In Peru, the Moche people worshipped nature and often depicted flamingos in their art.

In the Bahamas, the flamingo is the national bird.

In the Andean mines, miners killed flamingos and believed their fat to be a cure for tuberculosis.

How petty we are. How inventive. *How.*

*

Sometimes I want to make a point so badly that I forget I can just come out and say it, plainly. Other times, I know better.

*

I have lived with these regrets: I've never been in a greenhouse or held my breath the length of the Gulf coast, though I thought to try the latter. In Florida, I waded in waist deep water, stepped on something sharp. Maybe coral. Maybe sponge. I curled my toes around it and brought it to my hands. It weighed like fire in the scrub, like fire vanquished finally at high tide: immeasurable then? A nerve is not unwrapped if the engine that drives it, if the rise, if the laceration, if the every joyless effort has no proof: blossoms are something other than wounds.

*

Ideas. Wikipedia tells me that "Flamingos are very social birds; they live in colonies whose population can number in the thousands. The members of a group stand together and display to each other by stretching their necks upwards, then uttering calls while head-flagging, and then flapping their wings. The displays occur randomly. These displays stimulate 'synchronous nesting' and help pair up those birds who do not already have mates."

There's no connection between Curious George and flamingos, except there are exactly the same engine: curiosity breeds investigation begets rumination leads to sense. Perhaps. And this: both the male and the female flamingos feed their chicks with milk produced in glands lining the whole of the upper digestive tract.

*

College again. The same girl. We almost married. She tells me, *sorrow from far away is a kind of power.* I tell her, *between the spider and the jailbird, between the lover and the poet, between the friend and the body, I'll take the body.* But not really, because who speaks like that? But it's what I wrote down in my notebook. *I'll take the body* unfolded, the perfect ratio of grit to pillow.

And then she tells me, *this is the first I have washed my body since you touched my body.*

I want to wake up next to her even now: *I dreamed about the woods,* I'd whisper, but she'd turn away, feign sleep.

We invented a game called The Flat-Earth Theory of Love Affairs. It's a game where space and chaos figure out that coincidence is lonely. She always won. She'd lay on her back like a jigsaw, like the wrong tool from the wrong toolbox, a song played out of key, worrying smooth with her fingers her ear lobes, the porchlights drawing the lawn tightly around our apartment.

She whispers, *tomorrow I will learn a theory so dense it will send you into mourning.*

I whisper, *show me again how to take you home.*

*

Do the flamingos at Brookfield Zoo—I'm there, maybe 14 or
15, and I don't want to be there, but I'm there because my dad
said I should be thrilled to tour the zoo with my baby brother,
who's 5 or 6, and loves flamingos—who are wing-clipped and
grounded?—get jealous when the geese, in formation, fly overhead? Do the geese know they're making a shape instinct has
induced? The flamingos don't know I am watching them watch
the geese watch the horizon.

*

I want to understand *stillness* newly, anew, without the compli-
cation of *usually predicative* or *not sparkling or effervescent: a still
wine* or *obsolete (of a child) dead at birth*. Dictionary.com tells me
this, from John Ashbery:

> Such moments as we prized in life:
> The promise of a new day, living with lots of people
> All headed in more or less the same direction, the sound of this
> In the embracing stillness, but not the brutality,
> And lists of examples of lots of things, and shit...

Adverbial, too. *Do you still love me? I still don't know your
name. Sit still.* Poetic, dialectal: *always.* Often used with a com-
parative: *even or yet: still more insults.*
And shit.
And shit. That seems about right. Silent *or* calm, gentle *or*
quiet. Even: *subdued.* Wanting to feed the blackbirds off the deck
of Aunt Mary's cabin in Arbor Vitae, WI, felt like an exercise
in swift disobedience, contradictory malevolence, but really
the reason my father told my cousin and I not to feed them is

because then they would never leave, they would pester, they would come back *still* the next year. *Even then; nevertheless.* A sentence connector, the dictionary says. My cousin and I sling-shotted several of the blackbirds from the trees, but we never hit them square – they always flew away. The pump-action pellet rifle, however, was a different story. Seven pumps, level the sight, squeeze, *don't pull*, slowly, stop breathing, *compress* the trigger fully. And the birds would fall to the pine-needled ground. We'd swoop down the steps and chuck them into the lake, always hoping hopelessly to see a 40-pound musky surface to take our offering for a snack. I still daydream about this.

Poetic silence or tranquility: the still of the night.

To make or become still, quiet, or calm. Verb. Transitive: *to allay or relieve.* Our suspicions were stilled. The blackbirds, like the Sanskrit word for "immobile," *sthānús,* from which *stillness* derives, no longer could feed on our leftover waffles, but new blackbirds would arrive tomorrow morning when the waffles were hot once again, and we'd hold our breath as we aimed the slingshots this time to keep our bodies still.

✳

Did I mention we were going to marry? In a couple months. Rehearsal space: booked. Deposited. Nearly in full. Church and pastor: booked. Invitations nearly mailed. Registry – damn it those scanners are fun – completed. Her dress: purchased, hemmed, hemmed again (she kept losing weight: *it's most brides' dream,* she says, but she knew something else was wrong, something bodily, though it'd be years, and of little consequence to me, until she'd find out what), hanging in her mother's bedroom closet – to this day, eleven years later, I've yet to see a picture of it, though I still think I'd like to.

We've grown apart, she said. *We aren't kids anymore,* she said.

I think I need to do something (insert: some*one*) *else*, she said. She'd gone to Florida to an academic conference—she was in her first year of grad school studying linguistics, I was finishing my bachelor's—*danced* with a guy at a bar, decided maybe there was something, someone better. I know now, of course, that there was, or could be, or would be. A lot better. But that day—*I'm sorry, but I know this is what's right for me...I mean, for us*—in a booth at the local ihop—I was sure she was wrong.

Hindsight's funny. Or mean. Or adjectivally impossible to explain. But one thing it isn't? Possible to predict.

*

An 83-year-old Greater Flamingo, believed to be the oldest in the world, died at the Adelaide Zoo in Australia in January, 2014.

*

Recently in Madison, wi, authorities shut down a *snuggle house*. Patrons paid $60 "for an hour of g-rated contact—no funny business." The owners called it a *spooning space*. The authorities called it a *den of iniquity in disguise*. Yes. In disguise. g-rated contact: a handshake, a pat on the back (depending on gender, depending on age, depending on relationship), a high-five. Funny business: spooning under the covers, making love, fucking, an Eiffel Tower, fisting, double-fisting. The benefits of touch therapy have been proven once and again by modern science. *Increased oxytocin levels and a sense of well-being can last for days after a snuggling session.*

Should I be offended, complacent, or smug: "assistant city attorney Jennifer Zilavy said, 'No offense to men, but I don't know any man who wants to just snuggle.'" *No offense?* Whenever someone starts a commentary with *no offense*, they know they are about to make an offensive remark. But I don't begrudge the attorney. She's likely right. Our brains (or maybe our hearts?), as has been said, aren't always where they should be.

Flamingos hearts are generally larger, like all avian species, than mammalian hearts when compared to an animal of equal body mass. This adaptation allows more blood to be pumped to meet the high metabolic need associated with flight. The comparison begs. The way blood rushes, to extremities, during *snuggling*. Biology, like fate, is both cruel and unpreventable.

I keep thinking of this word: *blanketing*. Is this—potentially—illicit snuggling happening atop the covers? Beneath it? In a bed (or couch or floor) at all? I want to picture it. Voyeur? Sure, why not?

Flamingos usually copulate during nest building. During work. *Hi-ho, hi-ho, it's off....* Maybe it's this instinct. To build, to nest, to cuddle and snuggle and consume G-rated contact. Maybe.

Police, up until the final decision to shut down the snuggle house, were planning an *undercover snuggle sting*. But the owner finally answered their phone calls, made the necessity of the sting, well, unnecessary. The owner told the cops he'd outfitted each room with a panic button. And security cameras. Aren't we all voyeurs after all?

*

How thin the line between praise and censure. There are always things left unsaid that should remain so. And vice versa.

*

Maybe a comment on *what is found there*. Or some revelatory statement about beauty, whatever that is. I guess I'm pausing here, ending here, perhaps, and saying something about splendor or resilience or something less tangible, or more tangible. At a recent talk, poet and essayist Dana Gioia thought aloud: "*Beauty*, as a term, is quaint.... Beauty is the missing key to our culture.... The rehabilitation of beauty can only benefit our society.... Beauty is a thrill of pleasure. A disinterested pleasure; we don't want to possess beauty but merely be in its presence. Beauty leads to the most important human experience: joy." But we also know that *beauty is nothing but the beginning of terror* (Rilke), is ugly sometimes.

I'll always be a boy, *the* boy, the one who forgets frogs have innards colored independently of their skins, who wants to watch my baby brother watch the flamingos watch the geese and wonder *what is found there?* The big picture, right? The themes. What I've learned. *Want disguised as a mouthful of air. A den of iniquity in disguise. History in procession.*

Ideally, you are something other than. You are a question unanswerable, and the question is the engine that drives you.

WATER HAZARDS AND SAND TRAPS

So much comes close if you make of staying still a temple.
— CHRISTOPHER COKINOS

We were sixteen, knew how to load the backseat and trunk of an '88 Buick Regal with four-foot pieces of PVC – and elbow joints, tee reducers, connectors – rough-cut planks of plywood, reams of green AstroTurf, and hundreds of 18-gauge brads.

In the garage, a jigsaw (to cut ramps, holes, oases), hammers, a brad gun, space. Lots of space. We cut half-moon wedges from some of the plywood planks. Later, we'd nail cut-out plastic paint trays into the left-over space and fill the trays with water or sand: water hazards and sand traps. We punctured several holes in each piece of wood: different hole locations – covering the one not in use was as easy as a hinge, a piece of cardboard, and a few screws. Ramps, turns, inclines, declines. False fronts. Wedges, usually 2×4s, to block progress, *to impede*: delay or prevent; hinder. Once the layout was finished, we gunned AstroTurf to the exposed wood.

Then we'd break the thing down into pieces so we could install the PVC piping system beneath. This allowed us to sink our shot and have the ball return to us at the tee-box. This was unnecessary. It would have been just as easy to have the ball drop through the hole onto the concrete of the garage floor. We could retrieve it there. But the *returning*, the ability to bury a thing and have it come back. The golf ball always came back. Fathers

45

didn't always come back. Jared Diamond, in his *The Third Chimpanzee: The Evolution and Future of the Human Animal*, writes about how difficult it is to get accurate scientific information on adultery: people have many reasons to lie about their perceived transgressions. It's about *turning*, or *getting lost*. Scientists discovered that *interpersonal synchronization of stepping* happens when people walk-and-talk side-by-side. They don't know why this occurs, but it has therapeutic uses: injured subjects walked on side-by-side treadmills and chatted; the slower of the two started walking faster to keep pace with their partner. We lie to ourselves about our capabilities, our prudent silences—what's adulterous emerges.

Mom at work. Dad at work—and going home afterward to a different house. Step-dad newly dead of cancer. We built because our hands could do the work.

We built, over the course of that summer, a half dozen mini golf holes. Some took hours to build, others took weeks. We feared that, eventually, our designs might become too complex for our simple tools. We had one hole, however, left to build. It would be 24-feet long, possess four ramps, five levels, three holes (for variety, for levels of difficulty). It was to be our masterpiece. Naive, we were. But driven, too. We invited several friends to play it with us. One friend—as we putted, took turns subconsciously figuring πr^2 and *angle of approach*—told us about armadillos; we'd never seen one. According to our friend, armadillos have a defense mechanism where they hop in the air when frightened. The animals themselves are small enough to pass under a car unharmed, but when they see the car coming, they leap up in the air and are killed by the underside. He said, as his putt rolled back, again, down the final ramp, that he'd felt compelled to share that, for some reason. We didn't even know if it was true.

YOUR BODY MOVES YOU
THOUGH YOU WISH IT WOULDN'T

You were fifteen and had never been touched. Your friends, huddled together in Nathan Pitz's basement, couldn't understand and had taken it upon themselves to help. Most nights in that basement you drank Pepsi by the case (stole a bottle of something from a liquor cabinet when you could), watched Cinemax through the fuzz, and otherwise fucked around: ping-pong, video games, flirting.

One of the girls, a frizzy red-haired junior with a high voice and freckles over 100% of her body, had a reputation. Maybe like a madam, like a tour-guide-of-what-came-next.

*

You liked to be touched. The weight of someone caring. Your father's hand upon your head every other Friday night when he picked you up for dinner. Your mother's kiss on your forehead at bedtime, her hands kneading your thighs when growing pains and leg cramps kept you up all night. Your white house—a raised-ranch; full-basement; mother-in-law addition; two decks, one upper, one lower; a pool—at 121 Ann Street in Cary, Illinois acted as the pick-up and drop-off site for eleven years of shared parental custody exchanges. Duffel bags full of clothes, CDs, books, new toys, homework, candy, imagination, determination, blame.

You knew their divorce wasn't your fault, but you never said it aloud. You visited a therapist once. You don't remember his name, but his office, off First Street and Route 14, kitty-corner the Veteran's Park and Cemetery, just above the fishing pond where you learned to bait your own hook with crickets, stood four stories tall, the tallest building, by two stories, in all of Cary.

*

Your stepfather Jim's Glioblastoma Multiforme (GBM) developed, as it usually does, from astrocytes – star-shaped glial cells that support the nervous function of the brain. GBM generally kills within the first 15 months after diagnosis. It's fast. Almost as fast as pain, which travels through the body at 380 km/hr.

Disney World, 1994: you missed the Light Parade because Jim couldn't walk without falling to his left and was afraid to leave the motel. Prior to that trip, he'd been drinking two bottles of Maalox every day due to intense, undiagnosed cramping. Sometimes, he'd fall asleep on the toilet. Other times, he'd be awake with headaches and dizziness and vomiting. The doctors, though, couldn't figure it out – about 7,000 deaths occur each year because of doctors' sloppy handwriting. How many, you wondered, occurred due to mis- and un-diagnoses? They said *migraines*. They said *ulcers*. They said *hormone imbalances*. But after the Light Parade, your mom crying in the bathroom of the Motel 8, Jim asleep though he didn't mean to be, you and your sister watching *Gremlins* on the small color TV, Jim went to a neurologist. *Sophisticated imaging techniques can pinpoint brain tumors*. After one CT scan they knew what, years later, you think, your mom and Jim may have known – feared, anticipated, almost planned for? – anyway.

*

One night in Pitz's basement you lay in the elbow of the L-shaped couch. Stephanie, the red-head, cuddled next to you, her frizz tickling your neck, her breasts bra-less and visible in her low-cut v-neck. She wiggled purposefully. Her hand rubbed your thigh. She nodded toward the adjoining room. She knew you were incapable, knew it was a safe bet, knew you would never take advantage of her, but you didn't know that, not then, and not now. You wanted to. You wanted to. You needed to be enveloped and carried away, sucked and held. Kneaded and needed.

*

To lose your head. To explode. To be overcome. To overcome. This is what humans do. It's, mostly, who you are. You war; you reconcile. You fight; you fuck. You solve; you cause. You observe; you observe. Scientists trained flatworms to maneuver over a rough surface – on which they were initially uncomfortable – to find food. Once the trained worms acclimated to the surface, the scientists introduced untrained flatworms into the same scenario and observed, as expected, that the trained worms found the food much faster. The scientists then cut off the heads of the trained flatworms. The thing about flatworms: they overcome, regenerate, can lose – and regain – their heads. When their heads grew back, the trained worms still found the food faster than the untrained worms. Scientists have no explanation as to how this is possible.

*

"Do you know why you're here today?" the psychologist asked you.

"No." You spied several diplomas on his wall. You reclined on the leather couch—is this real? this isn't a movie? people do this?—your t-shirt riding up in the back, the cold against your skin.

The doc studied you as if you were some kind of puzzle he could put back together through telepathy, assuming, of course, that you needed putting back together to begin with. You remained unsure. The day before, your mom caught you pissing in the bushes in the backyard, and she yelled that you disgusted her, *what if the neighbors were to see you?!* You'd crouched there, swiveled your head to check for onlookers, and unzipped, fiddled with your cock a minute—blood pooled making it hard and impossible to pee—before realizing it best just to think of something else, so you closed your eyes and took a deep breath and pissed on the ground. The sizzle and slap-back of urine splashed the dried leaves. But it didn't seem a big deal. Come dinner time it had been forgotten. The talk over meatloaf and peas veered not toward your indiscretion but toward the typical *how was your day, fine, yours, good, thanks, what are we doing tomorrow, where's Jim, sleeping? puking?, oh, okay, we'll save him a plate, or maybe tomorrow will be better, maybe he'll be able to eat tomorrow or later, or never again, or don't worry, these things happen.* The guilt though, the drive to do it in the first place, scared you. The adrenaline. The worry. The threat of getting caught. It made you hard to think about doing it again—and you did it again the next morning.

*

In Wikipedia's entry on "Masturbation," under the heading "Health and psychological effects," there's this: *The medical consensus is that masturbation is a medically healthy and psychologically normal habit.*

*

Pitz's bedroom attached to the basement, so it was a short walk, one you'd been waiting to take with Stephanie, but not now, not here, not with what was going on at home. Jim questioned your mom and you every day. "Who are you? Where am I? Why are you here with me?" The tumor grew further into his hippocampus, up from the brainstem, it reached like a starfruit, bubbling and metastasizing past where surgery and chemo and radiation could go. He knew you one minute and then not the next. Mom tried to shelter you, but you knew. Pitz's basement was an escape. You whooped some ass on the Ping-Pong table, made out with your girlfriend-of-the-moment, flirted, drank, let your memory lapse.

In Pitz's bed, Stephanie looked at you: "We don't have to if you don't want to."

"I wanted to."

"But you don't now?" She kissed you. Soft and slow, her tongue.

All you could think, how sad, how sad, was *he's dying he's dying he's dying he's he's dying he's dying dying dying he's dying.* And you pushed her away, but not hard. You held her shoulders. And then you lay down together. In the dark. Five minutes. Maybe ten. Maybe more? You didn't know what amount of time was appropriate. All of the videos you'd watched, the old VHS tapes from friends' father's bedside drawers, hadn't prepared you for this.

After 15 minutes you stumbled back into the basement to cheers and hoots, the bright fluorescents illuminating your blush.

You never thanked her. You didn't know to thank her. It was enough to be in that room, the door closed, heat and dark and life and bodies. Beating. Beating. Your hearts and your youth.

*

You are controlled via impulse, via instinct. Your inner machinations give way to your outward sensibilities. Poet Graham Foust tweets: "Very anxious passenger next to me on flight back to Denver ripped pages from in-flight mag and made origami for all the kids aboard." We trust mostly ourselves, our loved ones, but control is all an illusion. In Churchill, Manitoba, it's unlawful to lock your car. Nearly 1,000 polar bears live in this tiny town on the north reaches of the Hudson River, and if one of them is hungry or aggressive, an unlocked car can provide a quick escape from the charging beast.

*

Noun. 1603. *Erotic stimulation...resulting in orgasm...achieved by manual or other...exclusive of intercourse.* Whatever the thing. Our bodies go missing. Whatever the thing you were looking for, it's maybe your hand, your mouth. When you need to know the time. The heat of the femoral pulse, how easy to slide your fingers. The last hour of spring, the first hour of summer: a scar, a seed clogging the surface of light and skin and you are not ashamed. You don't know the park. If a canvas – *you* is better as a verb. Skydiving and parasailing: a tether is the main difference. Thursdays after noon or Fridays after the kids go to bed. Write what you know. Learn your body what you don't. Your belly eats the wind. A man falls from a bell tower. A release. To escape. Manual or otherwise. Spread upward through his spine. He was the one who thought that given enough chances one man would, in mid-flight, in mid-destruction, grow wings. Our bodies go missing. You can't wait for others to agree with you. Once, your mother slapped you bare-handed.

"Are you afraid of anything?" the doc asked. You weren't.

Your 45 minutes ended much as it began. The waiting room. Grown men and women, some smiling, some not, some disheveled, some dressed too neatly, too cleanly – the woman with the full evening gown, dangly gold earrings, green high heels, her lips rouged to an unnatural color: she spoke demurely to the receptionist. You couldn't make out what she said, but it appeared of stately importance. Once back home, you never spoke of the therapist again.

For days, weeks, you thought about pissing in the bushes, about how the breeze tickled your skin, the relief of being in control, totally and without fear – the weight of caring about only yourself. Your body, your cock, your rumpled and incompleteness: untouched by hands that knew how you worked. Were you afraid of anything? Maybe of your own body, of what it couldn't do and what it could, and to whom. Of what you might do next with it, of what kind of touching might otherwise be forbidden if you stretched too far one way or another. If you found a secluded spot at school, just off the playground after the 3:00 bell, maybe you could find out, maybe you could touch yourself slowly, with unknown but precise purpose and without blame. Maybe you could harden in public, shame yourself, be open and closed and open and closed and open like the doors you sometimes dreamed about, door A and door B: one would lead you to the bed of some willing, hungry woman and the other to a mirror.

*

Alligators weigh only ounces when they hatch, but thirty-five years later – if they survive road-crossings, encounters with hawks and larger gators – they can be 11 feet long and weigh several hundred pounds. So why, while walking through the bayous of southern Louisiana, just outside St. Charles on a visit to McNeese State University – 2005, making a decision on an MFA program, newly married – on marked and unmarked trails, did you kneel inches from a full-grown prehistoric killer? He sunned himself just off the trail, his mouth agape, eyes closed. *Get closer, honey*, your wife cooed. *I want the picture to show scale.* Scale. His skin rippled in the sunlight; as you moved nearer him, you saw his musculature tense and flex beneath what looked like – and oh how you wanted to touch him – body armor.

You remember looking at the gator but also looking around. Wild flowers of colors unimaginable and yet somehow still furiously green – it was June after all. Vines crawled from the swamp and hung like tendriled appendages from the wood bridge up ahead. The swamp sang. Insects and birds and frogs and baby gators, all their music indistinguishable from the wind and one another. The periodic splash of something alive escaping from the green into the water. You wondered, did alligators sleep with their eyes open or closed.

To show scale. You got within several feet of the gator's snout, in front and to the right of him. You kneeled just long enough to force a smile and hear your wife snap the photo. *I think it's dead*, your wife said, as you reconvened some yards away from him and continued down the trail. But you knew he was alive. You had heard his breath, felt his breathing on your calves – though maybe you're imagining this now like how people who survive airplane crashes remember everything except the impact itself – seen his green-ridged and sloped back rise and fall. And the guttural hiss that filleted up his throat, a low rumble, a warning.

*

You aren't afraid of the body's totality but of its bridges, its cliffs, the way she reaches hesitantly to touch you, in the dark, in the light, or not at all. Probably not at all. The lack of attention is lonely, alienating. But the body's pleasures, its exhalations and inhalations, its shock and breath – the sinews of its twisting, its writhing. These are emotional needs met by your body's plain – an expanse, a prairie, a large area of land without trees – like in college when you learned everything you thought you could know of the body – the hours of exploration, how touching became necessary, tasting too, and it was who you were, all you wanted ever to be. You are, after all, a result of all your touchings. How to simulate

a lover's touch when your lover no longer loves you? You decide you must forego, then touch, and instead pick the nearest sense: sight. In the mail you receive a flyer for art classes offered at the local community center: Life Drawing 11. No prerequisite required. A warning: models are nude and your respect, professionalism, and tact are *required*. First come, first served. You decide you'll go. You arrive, that Tuesday evening – your wife thinks you're at your tennis league match – an hour early and are surprised to see a line already formed outside the classroom door. Once in the room, a semi-circle of chairs and easels crescent what looks to be a stack of cardboard boxes covered in blue velvet, though it's surely a couple of crates and an old throw cloth lit exceptionally well. The fourteen

of you pick your seats. You don't say much – whether its nerves or anticipation or some kind of mute sexual excitement, all of you portend adulthood fiercely. The teacher – a woman in her mid-50s, silver-haired, her knuckles veiny like a stream over rocks – tells you a bit about the class: *you'll each find an easel and a palette at your work station; please pay attention to line, shadow, shape; don't be afraid to stare, but do so respectfully and with intention to paint.* She then takes a seat at an easel and whistles loudly, calls for *Mark*. Mark

*

You wished they'd have found the tumor earlier, wished there were a name for the quiet in the living room when your mom told you the prognosis.

Your mom motioned for you to sit on the couch—the deep brown of the velvety fabric soft and warm against your thighs in the late summer swelter, the way the easy chair across the room, an odd but perfect match—its rich brown-sugar color offset with a floral design of yellow and orange—drew your eyes because you knew what she needed to say—no smile on her face, red rings around her eyes—was serious. She stood, arms crossed, a few feet from the couch. Jim stood near, and stared out of, the bay window at the front of the living room. His shoulders shook, but his crying was silent, heaving, unconstrained. They both, had they tried—had they been able—to make eye contact, would have been looking down to you. You'd never seen a man cry before—and maybe you haven't cried yourself since.

Years later, you read of the world's quietest room: it registers at -9 decibels. It's so quiet that you can hear your blood flowing in your own body. Maybe that's what you felt, what you heard, as your ears boomed and your eyes got hot. The silence of such a room can cause hallucinations. You wanted to fall asleep. You wanted to rest your head in the hollow of your folded arms, and be fast asleep, and be dreaming. It would be a simple dream—a dream of childhood and a dead-end street—and you would be both everywhere and nowhere in it. You would be the mind of the dreamer and the dream itself, the street and the dreamer of the street, and suddenly you would know this: you would have this dream, this exact sequence of *Car!* and *Game on!* and knee scabs and *Come home when the streetlight lights,* for the rest of your life.

*

You recently read an article about a student at Colorado State University that, according to deadspin.com, popped some molly prior to a Halloween party. Generally molly is an upper, a stimulant. It's a party drug, a rave drug. But the come-down can be hard and its effects are usually short-lived. This student though went on an "insane, masturbatory rampage." Your question: was the rampage insane or the masturbation insane? Or was the rampage masturbatorily insane? Commas. Adjectives. Compound issues therein.

The student's molly, police figured, was laced with something far more chemically unstable. He car-jacked an ambulance that he found parked out front of his dorm and joy-rode it down Highway 34. The police "found the ambulance...with several doors open, heavy front-end damage and fluid leaking," and it appeared "the driver...had hit the raised median, jumped the curb, hit a sign, went the wrong way and crossed back over the median before stopping."

The police found the student some 30 yards down the road, but he refused their commands to lie down and so they shot him with a stun gun; they found in his possession "a blanket, a cell phone and a box of Wheat Thins." Usually the sobering squad car ride to the precinct will squelch one's deviousness, but not this kid. Once at the station, the police observed that he "stood on a bench, kicked the wall, and masturbated."

There's something in the brain, a trigger, a switch that makes us unhinge.

*

Jim, after two years of misdiagnoses, no diagnoses—ulcers, leaning and walking inexplicably to the left then to the right into walls missing stairs into people legs don't stop why don't they stop my brain and my legs and my brain, puking, dizzy spells, headaches—and the doctors found a mass in his brainstem. Inoperable, mostly. They would try, though. They would eradicate some of the mass, radiate and drug the rest of it, maybe. A shaved head, prayers, MRI's for him. Nirvana, Pearl Jam, fourteen year old angst, flannel, hackeysack, skateboarding, "I'm on my time with everyone, / I have very bad posture," for you. You cared. Too much even. But you couldn't say it, couldn't think it clearly. The snapback of your Bulls' hat concerned you, the legs of that girl in Trigonometry concerned you, Jim's surgery concerned you. But all the same. Years later, you feel guilty for those preoccupations, for not knowing better the definition, diagnoses, details of Glioblastoma Multiforme.

What cut through: the hum of the hospital waiting room. You don't remember what the room looked like, what it smelled like, but you close your eyes and you can hear it. The drum of fear in your ears, the pulsing of a headache you didn't know enough to acknowledge, but even more the pastor's prayers—*God bless him, God lift him, God, glory to the Almighty God, bless this family and give them peace of mind*—the gurgle of the water cooler, the distraction of the vending machine—your coins kerplunking, chiming their way down the slot's throat, the muffled clunk of a Snicker's bar into the take-out port, the squish of a bag of Fritos.

Here's what you knew: he would die. Maybe not in surgery, but like some fire spreading to the shores of a lake, he would be extinguished when time said so. Here's what you didn't know: how to understand that information, how to hear it from your mother and the doctors and then do something productive with it. Even fear needs an image, something tangible for you to grasp hold of.

*

You wonder still whether the alligator, if he had wanted, could have snagged your leg, pulled you with him into the muck of the bayou. *You know*, you said to your wife, *gators can run damn near 40 miles-per-hour*. She shook her head, *no, they can't. Look at their little legs, they're too short!* But no, you'd read that over short, straight distances, they're extremely fast. *I could have died*, you suddenly realized and said aloud simultaneously. *I think he was sleeping*, she replied. That stopped you.

Your wife was suddenly twenty yards forward of you. Had you stopped or had she bolted ahead? She snapped photos of the wet mangrove trees and other grounded vegetation that hid the snout of another gator. *It's so green*, she said. *Have you ever seen anything like it?* You didn't know if she meant the mangroves or the gator, and you didn't care. She was right either way. What you saw? The gator's teeth. Even the soles of your tennis shoes wouldn't have stood a chance against the hard, gnarled calcium. You caught up with your wife and walked in silence over the bridge, watched the sunlight skim off the scum and muck, the black-pearled ringlets of a left-over splash – maybe a frog escaping. You spied a large-winged bird, maybe a heron, soaring above you. He soon found a place to land and splashed himself down. You watched him eat – or drink? – dip his long neck deep under the water to spear what appeared to be an adult mudfish. *Even the animals here without teeth are dangerous*, you said. Your wife snapped another photo and asked you, while staring at the great bird, *So, what should we do for dinner?*

*

strides in from the hallway. He's wearing a simple, white bathrobe, a sash tied around his waist. He looks to be about 25, is in shape though not exactly athletic, has brown hair buzzed close to his scalp. He's confident, or so his gait suggests. After taking a look around the room and saying, calmly, though to no one in particular, *thank you and please don't be shy*, Mark disrobes and reclines comfortably on the crate-cloth contraption, striking a modified *The Thinker* pose. The teacher: *have fun,*

folks! It suddenly dawns on you that you don't really know how to paint. But you have a pen in your pocket and figure you'll write some notes before attempting to give shape to the shape before you:

shoulders and the hollow of the shadows in skin that folds and unfolds at every breath

having hue, being hueless...no one is hueless?

the feet as braces to ankles

how one muscle leads to another

the snap-shut of the achilles

the body is made to fight, to excuse itself nothing

the heaving and rejecting the body must do to be whole

waists are forever

fists: child-like reminders of grasp and tug, food and food and food

we perceive curve as bulge – how we carry lumps

posture and violence aren't so different, are one action separated only by intent

the cock, always half-hidden, but it's the forward roll of the shoulders that haunts

shoulders don't begin or end

like hips, we've a place to hang

our filleted mass, equal parts base and sculpture

maybe we are born as shells

the body is a single curve

define body

a vessel, a captain, and a pirate walk into a bar

when Rilke wrote his torso, did he find it easy to surmise proportion?

waist and hips unwidened

two places to stare: the obvious (his cock...is it different than yours? bigger?) and the cut hollow between his waist and his hip, the short curve, the *man muscle* that leads to his lower back, and how, when desire finally catches and you feel flush, his lower back could hold enough water to drink

the body cannot launch, the body cannot upheave itself

without giving itself back to the ground

the body's purpose?

And now his presence seems overwhelming, his heat skin yours beads of sweat and a body is a body and a touch is a touch and your body is strumming thumping and you don't know if you can explain it and do you need to explain it and oh my god you'll have to eventually explain it to your two kids, that we have this body, all of us, for pleasure for pain for the times when those two things converge and oh my god we own this vehicle we mostly can't drive and so you step away from your easel and leave out the only door and down the hall and your body moves you though you wish it wouldn't.

*

Doctors performed a biopsy to ascertain both prognosis and treatment options. The analysis of tumor tissue under a microscope is used to assign the tumor name and grade, and provides answers to the following questions: 1) From what type of brain cell did the tumor arise? (The name of the tumor is derived from this) and 2) Are there signs of rapid growth in the tumor cells? You picture a doctor, a lab assistant, a grad student—who is qualified, who is confident–hunched over a microscope, a slice of Jim's brain–thinner than the thinnest thing you can imagine–on a slide. You zoom in as they do, the light from below the objective lens staging the sample as the mirror hones in on the cells, brightens what is otherwise invisible, makes large enough something small enough to kill secretly. You find, years later, a Manila folder with notes in your mom's handwriting. One of them reads like a script to deliver to loved ones on the phone: *The primary objective of surgery is to remove as much of the tumor as possible without injuring brain tissue needed for neurological function (such as motor skills, the ability to speak and walk, etc.).* The doctor said Jim's particular tumor was dangerous due to its location and the limited capacity of the brain to repair itself. Also, tumor capillary leakage, resulting in an accumulation of fluid around the tumor (peritumoral edema). Sometimes, science. Sometimes, bad luck. Sometimes, even wistful thinking. Caligula once ordered his troops to go to war with the sea. He made those troops return with seashells as plunder of war against Neptune.

GBM generally kills within the first 15 months after diagnosis. Fifteen months after his initial CT scan, Jim died peacefully in his sleep at a hospice care facility. The call came in the middle of the night. You heard the phone ring, waited for your mother's soft sobbing, rolled over and drifted back to sleep. You've never forgiven yourself. You kept beside your bed a copy of *The Guinness Book of World Records.* The next morning, you flipped it open and read the following: *Honey will never spoil. Because of its low levels of moisture and high acidity, you could theoretically eat ancient honey.*

*

You've never told anyone any of this, though that's how you know he's been getting your postcards – those tiny prayers you lift to him every night. On this night, you hope to dream both of him and of a solution to the busted toilet. These are the dichotomies of losing someone, because you don't know if you miss them or the way you felt about yourself when you were with them. Today you prayed about your least favorite words: *Proletarian, Bourgeois, Naked, Moist.* Outside, the trees snap in the November wind and you can't help but watch them dance. Without the pewter of a coming snowstorm, you don't know how to think *quiet,* how to practice *calm* and *tranquil.* The body is the plagiarizer you can't quite catch, the liar just quick enough to save face. The wonder of all this thinking is its noise.

LYRICISM OF THE FACT: AN ARCHIVE

In 2014, humans will take 880 billion photos. Every two minutes, we take as many photos as all of humanity took during the 1800s.

No US President has ever been an only child.

The fax machine, developed in 1843, was invented the same year people were traveling the Oregon Trail.

Some bowhead whales living off the coast of Alaska are well over 200 years old. They were born long before *Moby Dick* was written in 1851.

[We are never without loss for long, or grief.]

If the history of Earth were compressed to a single year, modern humans would appear on December 31 at about 11:58 PM.

[We think we tell stories, but often stories tell us.]

Pubic lice are endangered because of the popularity in recent decades of bikini waxing.

The woods take us into account – uncertain that falling never ends.

The only animal that kills from a distance.

Eight is the only cube that is one less than a square.

Next we learn from my wife of a disturbing incident: there is always something for which we are prepared to lose everything.

If you bid farewell to a friend while standing on a bridge, you will never see each other again.

[Staring is the predator's first weapon.]

AN EYE THAT NEVER CLOSES IN SLEEP: A NIGHTBOOK

Into the darkness they go, the wise and the lovely.
— EDNA ST. VINCENT MILLAY

I know the word: colic. I know the last waves of exhaustion held aloft, in a voice – not a story but the margins of what comes before *the end* or after *once upon a time*. Colique: French, pertaining or relating to the lower intestines – pain, discomfort, severe. From the Greek, *kolikos*. Knowing this proves nothing, but it gives the mind a place to dwell, a refuge.

I shawl her. I wrap her in pink blankets. Blue blankets. Green blankets. Sometimes I microwave a tube sock filled with black rice and rest it across her abdomen, think of heat on sore muscles, think *correlative*. But there is no answer, just the singularity of her discomfort, the night becoming its own erasure.

*

In my arms, baby girl, you are safe. In my arms, baby girl. We talk too much of legacy. Of feeling *home* when we say it. I read once that the dead are afraid of the living. We know the future controls the past, so weep now, baby girl, because you are safe, here, in my arms. The *O* of your mouth when you coo, the *O* of your mouth when you scream: they aren't so different, and neither is my touch, my *shoosh* or kisses to your skull-still-shaping. The tectonics below your skin – how like time it is to distinguish

69

the noise of your nights, to settle the weight I can press from my lips to you.

*

How often in one night can the lungs expand to secrete not breath but the fear of darkness human-born due to clenched eyelids – time-controlled night, of the setting, the forced quiet of the spectral: tenebrosity, that unlit gloom? In the womb, the omnipresence of dim, but now she's sombered, resigned to the nourishment daylight brings.

Secundus, that silent philosopher, wrote that the Universe is *an eminence ... a self-generated object of contemplation ... a nourishing ether, a globe that does not wander.* How holy. How prefatory, the ability to do anything because one first has to predict it.

Sleep comes, a fight that is not fought, because every language has its own silence even amidst its boom. The din, the fear of night or pain – it must be so confusing to have been born and given permission to *make*, light and dark, awake and asleep.

*

I don't think I've ever met an angel. Only the image of an angel can please us totally. Perhaps, in the shadows of headlights-through-trees projected onto my ceiling, I've seen – imagined – a new dream, a precious dream, *faith* – but the days are distinct and night has only one name: *prayer*. For the first three months of my Jorie's life, she suffered, and I prayed. If prayer is the most effective – and dangerous – form of repetition, an infant's screams of pain must be close behind. I remember holding her, wanting to hold her even closer, I remember breathing in pattern with her, gulping, my throat catching every time she stopped long enough to inhale – she vibrated, shivered, took

root deep inside herself. I couldn't counter her pain with sooth-
ing, but I tried.

*

Night: the part of the day after sundown and before sunrise.

    Day is a part of *night* like *fear* is a part of *terror*. It's only the
intensification that separates them.

*

I can think of no more essential terror: the faith of light, the
strange and persistent yawp amid realizing the day ends and
night ends and somewhere in the middle is the difference between the uncanny and the fear of abandonment. Realization
of such complexities isn't the half of it: *Experience*, Oscar Wilde
tells us, *is the name everyone gives to their mistakes.*

*

I half-remember Marian, half-remember the stories told years
later of how she watched me when my mom worked, how she
became the *other mother*. Marian had silver hair. Marian had
brown hair. Marian was sixty years old. Marian was forty years
old. Marian lived across the hall. Marian lived down the hall.
The apartment complex. Crystal Lake. The sidewalks, small
figure-eight pool – deep enough only to wade, or so the pictures
attest – the times I picked things up off the ground: a displaced
shingle from the roof; a dead robin, its eye sockets hollowed
to the bone, its feathers stiff with rain water and July sun; a
discarded popsicle stick; a bike pump that belonged to no one;
some old chewing gum; a pop gun, pointed directly at the camera. Marian recorded this boyhood mischief with snapshots

from an old Polaroid. She clicked the shutter button, shook the developing print, and put it in her back pocket to later give my mom.

The evidence: this entire cardboard box of Polaroids showing little boy hands holding little boy things, things either thrown away or left behind. During the long nights with Jorie, I sift mentally through these photographs, lose myself in the graying edges, the faded writing at the bottom of each Polaroid: *Gary, age four, pool, dead robin, why?* A recreation of moments too subtle as all memories return to time.

*

I wasn't alone those nights awake in Jorie's nightmare. My wife and her gentle *hush*, her softer hands across Jorie's brow, her slow rocking: the dance all parents learn early, practice when fathers pace the delivery room nervous, practice when mothers stretch painful ligaments. A slow swivel of the hips, loosed, unchained, a refrain, something wholly lost in, a making visible the moment of *attention*, of *affection*, and soon our bodies match the rhythm of our voices as our voices soften to flesh themselves.

I hoped to ease Jorie through the night, nothing more. Maybe set the stage, refine what I hoped for years later, explain through rocking, swaying, that I knew how to listen. I kept waiting for the moment when she'd become keenly aware of everything her body was doing to keep itself alive.

*

Peter Paul Rubens painted a father tearing, with his teeth, flesh from a son. *Saturn devouring one of his children*, 1637. The *O* of the baby's mouth, Saturn's hand gripped tightly to his sickle, his calves bulging, a black cloth covering what makes him him and his knee: a soft, clean place for the child's head to rest as Saturn rends and rips. The violence, the vertigo of stillness, how art captures and releases simultaneously our deepest. I think of art when in the arc of Jorie's screams because I read once, *Perhaps distraction at its most fruitful is a state of richest expectation.* But what am I expecting? Something infinite like silence or easement? Something of an unseen moment where I am not?

Rubens paints three distinct, gleaming celestial bodies above Saturn's head, to the right of his sickle: the planet Saturn and its moons, exactly as Galileo had described, and so the painting depicts not a father's wrath or degenerate's fucked-up hunger but rather an eloquent demonstration of influence, an astronomical mirror. Here Rubens *makes invisible the moment of renewal.* Here Rubens comments upon, distracts what's seen through what we can't un-see. The power of visible violence is that we can close our eyes to it, but we can't close our ears to screams without using our hands.

*

For four months I read American Literature. I don't mean some of it or *around in it* or even exclusively it. But all of it. From Columbus' journals to the ecstatic verses of Charles Wright, from Equiano's slave narrative to Faulkner's multiple narrators. I'd never before been immersed like that, and the light at the end? My Ph.D. qualifying exams. During those same months, Jorie screamed. At night, once my wife and son went to bed, I'd read, underline, highlight, absorb, recoil, bounce, obsess, laugh, and cry. I'd warm bottles, jostle Jorie on my knee keeping her balanced with one hand while I spined and read Cotton Mather's musings or Cummings' ekphrastic messes with the other.

When her screams became syncopated, when her tears turned dry and her cheeks reddened with heat, and I couldn't bare her pain any more than she could, I'd pack her in her car seat, cover her with a thick blanket knit by my wife's great-aunt, and put her in the back of the car. We'd drive, wait for the bumps, the dips and curves, the lights-not-lights-lights of neighborhoods, the streetlamp's punctuation of the car at night: the roving shadows of bare tree limbs and overpasses, the way they engulf slowly, first the front seat, then the back seat, then again and again. Winter-Michigan dulled us with its repetitions of silence and dark.

My wife and son safely asleep at home, and Jorie quiet, either asleep or mesmerized enough to forget to scream, to feel, we'd slalom the wet streets, the snowbanks and black-ice patches commonly unseen, but if you live among them long enough, you can anticipate them, see them in spite of yourself, feel the front axle's tug and pull and know well-enough never to counteract it, to roll with it, to let gravity be gravity. The road is wide when you don't fight it.

Once I sensed Jorie had relaxed or fallen asleep – parents know this trick intuitively: a distressed child rocked by the predictable motion of traffic will sleep the sleep of dreams – I'd make my way to Westnedge Ave, the main drag through central Portage and Kalamazoo, turn left, and pull into the deserted Home Depot parking lot. The lot, with its huge swath of open space, never-off lights, and good visibility to the outside world – we'd never go missing without a witness – made it a perfect place to park, to crack open again the spines of *Nature* or *Leaves of Grass* or "Sinner's in the Hands of an Angry God." For fear of distinguishing the vibration, the lull of car-sleep, I'd park around back of the store, keep the car running, the music low, the heat on, and I'd read while Jorie slept. When she'd start to wake, we'd do a few laps around the lot, pass the ghosted forklifts, stalled, never-started, left for anyone to take except, what would you do with it? Dumpsters full. Of what? Peeking through the lids: stray lumber, miscut 2 × 4s, sheets of ply broken or uncut or cracked, insulation pinked and wet from winter's spray of ice and rain and snow, sometimes an old truck tire or wires, cables, things salvageable on a nicer night. And soon she'd stop her stirring, settle again.

Sometimes I'd crawl into the backseat to sit next to her, angle myself to catch the streetlights on my book without spraying the remnants of them off the white pages into Jorie's eyes. Watching her chest rise and fall, reading *for every atom belonging to me*, and I could taste the blossom, the Oversoul, Nature, what it meant to think *holy*, to see the language leave my lips silently in the rearview mirror and reflect back empty, meaningless outside context, outside the silent conversation my eyes had with Jorie's breathing. Language tastes like salt hills, like the sweat it takes to make it. A sleeping child. Until finally I am sated and she is rested, and I remember, yes, wanting to be palpable, useful to something larger, and so I read on tired and full with something like assurance.

*

To hold something. Dearly. As important. As if your life. But we have to let go, too. Eventually. Dr. Ken Canfield, author of *The Heart of a Father*, writes about how to resuscitate an estranged father-daughter relationship thusly: *Ask your daughter to name three ways you can support her in the coming year.*

1) To *support*: bear all or part of the weight of; hold up. A list of things I'll never say to my own kids because I heard them too often as a child and couldn't understand them even then: Because I said so. Are you trying to light up the whole neighborhood? What did your mother say? Are you okay to drive? I'm not

okay to drive. No story tonight; we'll read two stories tomorrow night. How many times have I told you? Money doesn't grow.... Do I look like I'm made of money? On trees. We don't have to tell your mother about this. As long as you're living under my roof.... Ever. I'll treat you like an adult when you start acting like an adult. Payback's a bitch. Stop acting like your father. Like a girl. Like your mother. When I was a kid.... That's just stupid. One, two, two-and-a-half, two-and-three-quarters.... I'll give you something to cry about. This hurts me.... Don't make me come back there. More than it hurts you. You're going to poke your eye out. Seen, not heard.

The problem: who said what? Parent or child? And when?

That's for me to know and you to find out.

2) Dr. Canfield: *When a father abandons a relationship with his daughter she can become frozen in time relationally with the opposite sex.* "Placed on the other side of." "Contrary." "Standing against, opposed." "Set at odds with." I want to teach her that *opposite* is outdated, that the concept is self-defeating. But I can't. Because it isn't. Outdated, I mean. Elias Canetti writes, *There is something insane about the demand that everyone must gather by himself the articles of his thinking and believing; as though everyone had to build by himself the town he lives in.* It takes a village, my grandmother used to say. Rebuttal: every village has an idiot. So we want to teach our daughters how to remain unfrozen *relationally*, but how do we teach what *relation* means, what *sex*, and why *opposite*? Canetti again, this time paraphrased, *Of all the words I know in all the languages I know, no word is as concentrated as the English word "I."* And from that platform we teach *relationships*, we teach *worthwhile* and *happy* and hope not to abandon, hope not to distill a message dependent on binaries? Politics. Who we want (to be, to date, to abandon) has little to do with who we are and a lot to do with definition.

3) The three toughest things for any father to tell his children:

"I am sorry." "Will you forgive me?" "I was wrong." *Studies show that men tend to spend more time with their sons growing up than they do with their daughters.* I want, of course, to buck this trend, to be aware of it while simultaneously relegating it to my subconscious so that I don't *spend* time but spread it, enjoy it, forgive it its passing too rapidly. To satisfy myself, the kids. Something larger? (Again, I come back *here?*). *Satisfaction may be described as an internal affect resulting from the acquisition of pleasure and/or avoidance of pain.* Avoidance of pain. Yes. Ideally pleasure comes purposefully: I take Jorie apple picking; I take Auden, my son, to a basketball game; I take Jorie and Auden to the zoo, to see the giraffes, the elephants, the scorpions; I take Jorie to Gymboree; I take Auden to Gymboree. I take, I take, and I hope they take, something away or something to heart. *Regardless if the relationship is healthy or not, it still has some sort of effect.* But it has to fulfill, be fulfilling.

*

This essay should have begun with a grasshopper because it'd been a long time since I'd seen one and then I did, in the backyard today, voluptuously green, greener than the green grass and green weeds. I followed him into the trees, deep into grief, or loss, or nothing at all. And we watched each other. I could have grabbed him, held him in my cupped hands, and he'd have been silent, perhaps agitated and annoyed, but his noise, the stringed instrument of his legs, couldn't have sung in the cramped space between my palms. But I didn't grab him. I didn't stare at him for long. Instead, I walked back to the porch where Jorie was sitting crisscross-applesauce, grinding a piece of sidewalk chalk to its nub, scribbling big green circles, darkened and formless, telling me, "Daddy, I'm drawing you. Wanna see?"

IT'S JUST A BEAR, ASSHOLE

after Nick Lantz's "How to Write a Poem"

Start with *you are not Don Juan*. Start with *yes, I am*. Answers before questions. Start with the ladybug beats its wings eighty-five times per second. Start with sawdust and cats sneezing. Start with a woman giving birth in the back of a Nashville taxi on live TV as Sheryl Crow sings "All I Wanna Do" in the park across the street.

*

Aristotle said, *The aim of the wise is not to secure pleasure, but to avoid pain*. Start with we are in pain. Driving down Hamilton Church Road, my wife and I see a woman running along the median with a white sheet, the wind billowing it behind her. In the center of the road, blood all around it, lies a dog, its hind legs twisted, its tongue on the pavement. We slow and ask if she needs help. *No, I'm just moving her to the side of the road.* She wraps the dog and puts her in the grass. My wife sobs quietly but uncontrollably. This is how I know I love her.

*

Start with the first and only dream you've had of heaven. Aristotle said, *Mothers are fonder than fathers of their children because they are more certain they are their own.* Start with children – as long as you don't teach your own wisdom.

Try to walk to the first day of Spring. In the movies there's the Law of Children: they always walk faster than the adult accompanying them, and that's when they disappear.

*

My grandfather's first name was Woodrow. First names and the names of lakes I've fished always remind me of the cars I've driven, the women I've never slept with, the time I planted sixty-eight tomato plants in one afternoon because my grandmother said, *this corner of the yard gets more sun than a Hollywood hooker.*

And I believed her. After that, what's left to question? How often do we end our days with a meal and a kiss, turn onto our sides, and close under the heed of the evening news? What's more terrible: *Ten slain in Alabama, Stolen painting found by tree,* or me in the garden digging shallow pits, being careful to plant them deeply enough to encourage the growth of their roots.

*

If she cries, you cry. Start with that. It will be the first view you have of your life.

*

A man walks into a movie theater and shoots up the crowd. A man walks into a shopping center and shoots up the crowd. A man walks into a high school and shoots up the crowd. A man walks into a post office and shoots up the crowd. A man shoots up and walks into the crowd.

＊

The longing of the wounded to be the warning.

＊

Start with the flood of '93. You asked your parents if you could help sandbag the shores of the river – the idea part humanitarian part this-girl-you-liked-was-going – of course, they said no, but that girl, those people heaving fifty pounds from their shoulders to protect carpets and TVs and photos and deck footings because without them you'd sink. Without them you sank. The water towed under many.

＊

Start with winter-woods. Start with leftover bits of church-wood, food for termites and loners alike – bare-twigged trees a February wind can't shake, their limbs wet-dark with snow, are ghostly, are arithmetic, are what simple people fear most: we gather in our palms, like so much ash, all that's left to gather.

＊

Even the Puritans knew better than to tempt perfection, than to venture too deeply into the woods alone.

＊

Things drop from me: whole countries of time and lemons, lists of lists, and silent movies about lakes. What I love about lakes I love because, like baseball or syntax – Richard Hugo said, *truth must conform to music*, and that's true, but what he meant to say was: *it's okay to be hungry, just don't eat the dog or the celery*.

*

In the woods west of here, a man claims to have met Bigfoot outside his RV: *He threw rocks at my windows, broke my headlights. Yes, it was a "he." His forehead sloped bowl-like, and the females, their foreheads are more flattened, less concave. That's why I always park at the bottom of the valley. The males' brow hangs too low for them to see much uphill, and they are the curiouser of the genders.*

Somewhere between animal-consciousness and human-consciousness, a different physical dimension: *he eats, he sleeps, he poops, he cares for his family, and he broke my windows, but I'm not mad at him.*

I respect the gift of his presence. For the Iroquois, the Sioux, and Hopi, the Bigfoot is a spirit meant to convey a message: if you see the *Chiye-tanka*, or "elder brother," a husband to *Unk-ksa*, "Mother Earth," you touch him, you bring home his blessing to your family – the closer the kinship, the stronger the bond, both spirit and real being, *he can glide through the forest like a moose with big antlers, as though the trees weren't there. I know him as my brother.*

Start with sightings, decades old: Two boys witness a tree pushed into a river by a human-like being while fishing near Grassy. A fisherman finds a possible footprint on the Flathead River near Paradise. *Bigfoot lives near water, perhaps eats fish.* Start there. A deer hunter has a late afternoon sighting through his rifle scope on the same weekend that a father and son are approached by three large bipeds while hiking at dusk west of Asbury. A ginseng hunter recalls being terrified by a nighttime visitor on an old mining property: recall everything, take photos, remember the threat of starvation, the potential of appearance and disappearance. In this we are not alone. Besides: *it's just a bear, asshole.* Start with that.

"...the inability to isolate a sensation..."

Formlessness is form complete. In other words, sound the trumpet. In other words, form on its way toward resolve: sound the trumpet. On the farm. At the track. Image: *an intellectual and emotional complex.* The boy picks up the book on magic and reads it at night under the covers by flashlight.

But don't be afraid to make a point. Image is character. Image as character. Image as form. Formlessness. The poem as a geometry of fear. Or longing. Or both. *I've been working on the railroad....* Nothing wrong with plotting – plodding – an image. Poem is work. The poem as canvas. Is. There's always some new way to make metaphor worry itself thin.

Art is lonely = Lonely is art. Until viewed. No poetry, of course, without a witness. Once, in college, I saw a man fucking a woman behind the Quiznos. I watched for three minutes. And then it was over. The minutiae of passion, in passion, makes passion palpable.

What bursts in the very moment of bursting is image. Gustaf Sobin.

The poet's charge is to *look* – inward, outward, over, under, after, per, through. To use the world of the preposition actively. To help us see. It's not enough, however, to describe. We must inhabit. It's perspective. Viscerally.

Without *present.* With *presence.* What we see (or sense in any way) is always in relation to something else prepositionally. It's how we relate; it's how we intuit; it's how we make the world. How we make the world makes us make the world. How we arrive in brushstroke, in verb. Everybody is never always naked, or never fully clothed.

Often times there is weakness in trying too hard to say something unusual. A tree that flowers but bears no fruit. *What we see clearly is not perhaps the heart of reality toward which the image leaps, but the quiet attention that is the form of the impulse to leap.* Robert Hass.

It's been suggested (Rukeyser) that a poem involves a sense of arrival. We leap to arrive. We write to arrive. We sleep to arrive. We mark growth from one image to the next by how we arrive. It's imagination we express—an interdependency between expression and arrival. Unconscious (sleep) versus conscious (not-sleep). We imagine in both states. We express in only one.

Time ceases to exist. It takes less than a minute to read a short poem, but the reverberation felt in, of, about, around, after (again, the prepositional) lasts much longer. The other day, this. Out the window over the sink, I saw the neighbor kids laughing and playing in full firemen costumes. It was raining. The *erotic double*, we say. Thank you, we say.

He says he doesn't feel like working today.
It's just as well. Here in the shade
Behind the house, protected from street noises,
One can go over all kinds of old feeling,
Throw some away, keep others.
                    The wordplay
Between us gets very intense when there are
Fewer feelings around to confuse things.
Another go-round? No, but the last things
You always find to say are charming, and rescue me
Before the night does.

John Ashbery.

My wife takes too many pictures, and they're peppered about the house. They're mostly all terribly composed. Some of them have celestial blurs of light where her fingers meet the flash. Never by yourself alone. No audience is present in the making.

Oftentimes we try too hard to say anything. I heard a story about a deer and a bear, best friends. The bear would bend down the bough for the deer to reach the fruit. We all reach the fruit because someone bends down the bough. Right?

"The only people I trust," my grandfather once told me, "are fishermen. And I don't really even trust them." The future tense is impossible. The elimination of death. Consequence. Another story about my own life. It's the end of gesture. The end of concern.

Where the river meets the rain, the body fails the treeline. Or something like that. Nature is also impossible. *No water drinker ever wrote a poem that lasted.* Horace. Days and nights go by in silence. Such is the word: writing. Detached from everything, including detachment.

Love set you going like a fat gold watch. Plath. We all fall in love once. We all keep time. The root poe- comes from *grass, a grassy place.* In a field then, we live. In a field of prairie grass, cattails or milkweed or riverbank rye, chairmakers rush, where we might congregate, where we might roll in the wool grass. But why? In a word: sensation. In a word: image. In a word: poetry.

As a child, I saw a man, smiling, throw his wedding ring off a bridge into the Fox River. I witnessed. In a word: *in-an-instant-of-time-we-find-something-else-to-say.*

ON WHINING

Yesterday, you and your son took a magnifying glass[1]–a good one you bought at a hobby store–into the backyard to look at the leaves of romaine growing in your vegetable garden. You wanted to see the veins, the holographic chutes of chlorophyll, the way light splayed through the cuticles. Instead, you discovered a common garden slug, a big one.[2]

You peered closely, caught the light in the glass. The foot, the foot fringe, the mantle, the tail. The respiratory pore, or the *pneumostome.* Two kinds of tentacles: the ocular, or optical, depending on the guide you use, and the sensory: *what an oxymoron!* Isn't sight a sense already? Why name it thrice? Your mother-in-law: *yes, it's a sense, but so are smelling and hearing.* An exchange between a father and a son and a magnifying glass and a garden slug interrupted. She'd come out to the back porch to smoke. Again.[3]

Your mother-in-law lives with you and knows everything.[4]

---

1   Eula Biss, in "It Is What It Is," writes, "*Experimental* once meant 'based on experience as opposed to authority.'"
2   You're talking as a bat navigates. Not to hear yourself but to know where you are.
3   Brian Greene, *The Hidden Reality*: The passage of time depends on the particulars–trajectory followed and gravity experienced–of the measurer.
4   Sometimes you are the symptom and the cause. But you must prefer one over the other. Both point to the fact that you are, always, healing.

What the neighbors had for dinner.

How to discipline your children.

Why to discipline your children.

Why Iraq will never be a democracy.

How Jeremy Wade will finally catch an epically sized arapaima in Guyana.

What best to eat to lose the last five pounds of subcutaneous belly fat.

How to best clean the grill grates.

And she'll tell you all of it, for free, by listening in on every conversation you have.

Is this a critique? A whine? A bitch? Yes. But *it* is also free. Are you perfect? Not even close. Are *you*? No, *you* aren't either.

Your mother-in-law is a meteorologist, an entomologist, an ichthyologist, a grandmother and a damn good one.[5]

The slug, with just your eyes, is slimy, slick, looks like it might be hard to hold in your hand. But go ahead, pick it up and rest it in your palm. It's actually tacky, a bit like damp silly-putty or modeling clay. In the magnifying glass, its skin is pearly, almost translucently patterned, milky, textured. Your son flips it over in your hand and you find: The mouth is located between and below the sensory tentacles, *and is equipped with a radula, a tooth-covered rasp that the slug uses to grate plant tissue.* The slug glides along a path of mucus that is secreted by the pedal gland, located just below the mouth. In this position, you can see the pneumostome pulse with breathe-in, breathe-out. What a wonder the world is when zoomed-in upon.[6]

5   The folder where you keep your in-progress essays is a Mead FiveStar with conversion tables in one pocket insert and *Useful Information* lists in the other. A dekagram equals 10 grams. One gram equals 0.002 pounds. *Table of Circular Measure.* 60 seconds = 1 minute = 1 degree = 1 meridian = 69.16 miles of the earth's surface. *Table of Avoirdupois Weight. Table of Surface Measure.* An acre measures 208.7 feet on each side. *Multiplication Table.*

6   Has anyone ever written a catalog of gestures?

You're following these observations back to yourself, back to where you started. There are so many things to consider looking away from, but this can't be one. But how do you, when sharing a roof, deal with conflict without upsetting balance, especially when that balance hinges on shared governance, on love, on other roof-sharers' well-beings? So you read, "15 Ways to Deal with a Difficult Mother-in-Law," and feel guilty the entire time—*maybe she's not the difficult one.* Maybe you are. *You are entitled to a peaceful life,* warns (says, writes, mentions) one article.[7]

The taxonomy of a thing or being. Its description and physiology and ecology and behavior: all add up to make a slug a slug, a mother a mother. There's always *further reading* and "How to Deal with an Obtrusive Mother-in-Law" and "Quick Fixes for Difficult In-Laws" and "Ten new complete mitochondrial genomes of pulmonates and their impact on phylogenetic relationships" in *Evolutionary Biology. You have to distance yourself physically and remember that it's highly unlikely anyone will change.* That seems like an invitation, an evocation, a hymnal sung by a man already defeated. You try to *distance yourself physically* and *understand the common problems,* but she *is* the common problem. So you detach yourself, emotionally, physically, try to share a roof but not a room. That works. For a time. But then you feel badly. She's not a bad mother; in fact, she's a great mother, an even better grandmother, but damn it,

---

7   Brian Greene, *The Hidden Reality*: Quantum mechanics broke the mold of the previous framework, classical mechanics, by establishing that the predictions of science are necessarily probabilistic. We can predict the odds of attaining one outcome, we can predict the odds of another, but we generally can't predict which will actually happen.

she knows *everything*.[8] She listens, intrudes, can't sit quietly by while you and your wife discuss your day, the news you heard about friends, gossip you learned about celebrities, talk about that movie you saw once – and from the other room: *Wait, you mean the one with the guy that cures that disease?*

How Sochi won the 2014 Olympics over other, more-qualified, cities.

Why Putin is a *puritanical dickhead*.

How many calories are in a large red delicious apple – okay, you concede this one as it's fairly common knowledge.

That Ashton Kutcher and Mila Kunis have been dating secretly for months.[9] Why you have no right to criticize your wife for the money she spends haphazardly.

	1	2	3	4	5	6	7	8	9	10	11	12
1	1	2	3	4	5	6	7	8	9	10	11	12
2	2	4	6	8	10	12	14	16	18	20	22	24
3	3	6	9	12	15	18	21	24	27	30	33	36
4	4	8	12	16	20	24	28	32	36	40	44	48
5	5	10	15	20	25	30	35	40	45	50	55	60
6	6	12	18	24	30	36	42	48	54	60	66	72
7	7	14	21	28	35	42	49	56	63	70	77	84
8	8	16	24	32	40	48	56	64	72	80	88	96
9	9	18	27	36	45	54	63	72	81	90	99	108
10	10	20	30	40	50	60	70	80	90	100	110	120
11	11	22	33	44	55	66	77	88	99	110	121	132
12	12	24	36	48	60	72	84	96	108	120	132	144

9   You didn't realize there were so many kinds of theoretical physics: relativistic physics, quantum physics, cosmological physics, unified physics, computational physics. All of them lead scientists to believe that perhaps there is no universe but instead a multiverse.

What breed the neighbor's dogs are.

How best to foster a caring, nurturing home-life for your kids.

She doesn't, however, listen fully. Just the other night, while in the kitchen washing dishes with your wife – a ritual you two use as a ruse to spend a few minutes alone: you wash, she dries – you told your wife how much you loved Hamlet's line, "I could be bounded in a nutshell, and count myself a king of infinite space." From the other room, your mother-in-law, above the din of the television, the barking of the dog, the hum of the refrigerator, chimes in: *Wait, wasn't it Shakespeare who said that?*

Back in the garden, the slug, in all its lack of speed, meanders across the flesh of your thumb pad. You learn that a slug's body is prone to desiccation, which explains finding it on the freshly watered romaine leaf. Generally they confine themselves to the moist retreat of second level soil during daylight – and at night, you find them, when you take the dog out before bed, scaling the humidity soaked vinyl siding.[10]

Slugs must generate the mucus you so generally associate with them in order to survive. It's foul-tasting and so thwarts predators. It's also sticky and helps them maintain grip on the substrate as they feed.

Your son: *Can I hold it?*

---

10 Brian Greene, *The Hidden Reality*: think of two clocks, one on the ground, the other on top of the Empire State Building. Because the ground clock is closer to the earth's center, it experiences slightly stronger gravity than the clock that's high above Manhattan. General relativity shows that because of this, the rate at which time passes on each will be slightly different: the ground clock will run a tiny bit slow (billionths of a second per year) compared to the elevated clock.... objects move toward regions where time elapses more slowly; in a sense, all objects "want" to age as slowly as possible. From an Einsteinian perspective, that explains why an object falls when you let go of it.

Before you can even answer, your mother-in-law: *Sure, go ahead!*[11]

You: *Yes, son. Go ahead.*

You want to watch him register the tactile sensation, watch his eyes widen or narrow, his lips grimace or smile, his hand remain still or jolt in slimy anticipation, but before you can witness any of his reactions, your mother-in-law: *What's it feel like? Is it slimy? Do you want to put it down? You can put it down, you don't have to hold it. What's it feel like?*[12]

One article suggests that *If all else fails, relocate to another city.* As if it's that easy. As if it's that big of a problem. Maybe you're lucky. Maybe her attention, her intrusive listening, talking, parenting-when-she-shouldn't is actually helpful? She is, after all, loving and attentive, generous and kind, anxious to please and willing to help.[13]

But she isn't your parent. You are on equal terms, and that's what makes it awkward. You can't criticize her precisely because you don't have the history with which to do so. Ten years does not make a lifetime, does not make a parental bond. And so you breathe deeply, distance yourself, remember the good far outweighs the bad, *remember it's highly unlikely that she'll change* (this one appears in every article), attempt to change yourself—because if it isn't her, it's you.[14]

11 They say hypnosis only works if you believe in it, but a friend told you that slugs taste, once grilled over hickory wood by the dozens, like mussels.

12 You knew a guy in college who when he got nervous would repeat the beginning of compound words over and over again under his breath.

13 No experience is complete until you tell yourself about it later, once the facts and fictions become interchangeable. Science tells us that memories change over time as we tell, shape, retell, and reshape experience into narrative.

14 After a poetry reading where you read new work, work that revealed you, a listener told you, *I really wish you'd put more of yourself in your poems.*

"How to Avoid Escalating the Conflict," Rule #8: *Think about your spouse and child. Don't say or do anything before taking a break and letting the tension diminish. Sometimes you simply must bite your tongue.*

You call your best friend for advice. *Fuck her. She's already making your life miserable. Tell her so. What do you have to lose?*

You call your dad to ask for different advice. *Remember, son, you will catch far more flies with honey.*[15]

---

15   Brian Greene, *The Hidden Reality*: In the far reaches of an infinite cosmos, there's a galaxy that looks just like the Milky Way, with a solar system that's the spitting image of ours, with a planet that's a dead ringer for earth, with a house that's indistinguishable from yours, inhabited by someone who looks just like you, who is right now reading this very book and imagining you, in a distant galaxy, just reaching the end of this sentence.

/

LYRICISM OF THE FACT: AN ARCHIVE

Definition of *discernment*: when nine miles into a twelve-mile run, you spy the turkey vultures in the treetops.

[Purpose] [General Project Information] [Lessons Learned] [Administrative Closure] [Open-Ended Action Items]

When you're driving down the road and several wrens are attacking, mid-air, mid-dive, mid-tumble, a red-tailed hawk.

All the matter that makes up the human race could fit in a single sugar cube.

That makes me feel like a fool.

[I very much like to be the fool.]

There are several parts of a bird's body, my five-year-old son tells me, and *they all lead to its mouth.*

The Great Pyramid was built circa 2560 BC, while Cleopatra lived around 30 BC. The first Pizza Hut opened in 1958, which means Cleopatra lived closer to the deep dish supreme than to the Pyramids.

[No matter where you go, there you are.]

The parachute was invented 120 years before the airplane.

[Foresight: rummaging, the horizon–this is how it works around here.]

A bee produces only one-twelfth of a teaspoon of honey during her entire lifetime.

In the sixteenth century, Turkish women could divorce their husbands if the man failed to keep his family's pot filled with coffee.

THERE ARE MANUALS FOR THOSE

An excess of facts leads to fiction, but an excess of photographs leads to facts. And I have plenty of old photographs.

It would have been May or June of 1979, the early summer, the humidity not yet enough to force them from their cramped apartment, not enough to keep them in the living room at night, facing the box fan, the only fan in the apartment, all night, every night, sleeping nude or in underwear, each curled up against an arm of the old wood-framed, flower-upholstered, hand-me-down couch. Love gave way to survival, as it so often does.

During the day, he studied and she worked two and three jobs, dead-end jobs at dead-end places in dead-end towns: Frankie's Laundromat, some desk job, some other desk job. He studied deciduous teeth, molars, compaction, the complexities and severities of gingivitis, how to compose a business budget, how to buy life insurance, *why* to buy life insurance. He was practical. And busy. And she left each morning, came home each night, exhausted, but not too exhausted.

He had so much hair. A floppy 1970s mop-on-top and a full beard, red and brown and brown some more. Her long locks lay braided down her back. Her complexion soft and simple, but vibrant, eyes like pockets.

The pictures of the living room prove she, even then, vacuumed a checkerboard pattern, an outfield crisscross into the rug. Details, they say. Details.

They didn't need a child yet. There was no money, only debt. There was no space, only one bedroom. But soon. A father and a mother. A son. The rhythms of their exhaustions matched one of those late spring days before the depths of summer's humidity swept them from their bed where they could be together, and sometimes that's all it takes, a mutual understanding that *today* is as good as *someday*.

*

The wreckage of misguided decisions comes only later. Hindsight and foresight. Ass and mouth. Your foot. Metaphors exist so fathers can calm mothers, so mothers can curse fathers, so sons can blame themselves.

*

He said, he said, *my son*: the noise sons make following their fathers.

I answered to *my son*. Or my name. Or both, at the same time but never my name first.

I didn't have just a father or just a dad. I had trips to Brookfield Zoo, the Shedd Aquarium, third-base seats at Wrigley, airshows, fireworks displays, circuses, carnivals, The Taste of Chicago. What I needed: help with my homework, dinner, clothes, a ride to and from soccer practice, someone to hug my mom, tell her everything would be okay. Everything would be okay, okay?

How to reconcile, for a ten-year old, the responsibilities of a man trying his damnedest to raise a whole family only half of the time?

The dictionary: *Father*, from the Old English "fæder." "Pater,"
Indo-European. "An early form; a prototype." *A leading man.*

Okay, I could work with that.

My father: "A man who raises a child."

My father: "A male person whose sperm unites with an egg,
resulting in the conception of a child."

Me: "A male ancestor."

My Father: used as a title of respect.

My Father: to acknowledge responsibility for.

My Father: a male who originates something.

My Father: to act as father to.

My Father: See also, mother; parents.

Creation. Origin. Found. See also. A male parent of an animal. Forefather. Any male acting in a paternal capacity. Miso-
paterism (though not really). Begetter. Daddy. Old man. Sire.
Engender. Make. A mess.

Honour thy father.

*

The summer I discovered I had a body I also discovered I didn't
know what to do with it. I was ten. Fifth grade Sex Ed told me I
had a penis, told me it made life, told me not to make life, but it
didn't tell me the holiness of pleasure.

The boy across the street would come over and we'd swim or
trade baseball cards and then we'd be in my closet, on the floor,
on top of one another, fully-clothed. And we'd breathe. We'd
switch spots. Eventually my dick would twitch and something
like relief and shame and ohmygod chills would run from my
toes, and sometimes the arch of my foot would cramp.

I don't remember shame or confusion or anything but joy
and wonder. My body had purpose, had been purposed and
pleasured and plugged in for the first time. Like many boys, I

suppose, I couldn't get enough of myself: in the pool, the bath-tub, the bathroom at school, the back of the family station wag-on on the way to soccer practice. I didn't talk about it, was never caught – until years later – couldn't understand the sensations and so didn't try. I fell and fell and fell in love with my body.

*

My father left when I was four. My mother, full of guilt or pride or fear or hate or love. The spring before I discovered my body in that childhood closet, my father had a son. With another woman. Maybe I was scared. I remember the hospital, I remember not understanding all of it but knowing that being allowed there was special.

I wasn't allowed in the birthing room. My grandparents played checkers with me, I read a magazine, I waited in the waiting room. I didn't imagine then but imagine now the thick blue veins pulsing on my just-born brother's temples, the doctor's fingers in his throat, the hush in the room before he discovered his voice and scared himself alive. A couple hours later I watched his body fill with blood. And then when I held him, the way he stretched muscles in his face, made peace with breathing. How his body flexed and then went soft. He had so much hair. And the world was new. I overheard the nurse say that the woman in the next room pushed so hard she shit her-self, and her husband's laughter rolled down the hallway.

These aren't excuses. Only connections.

*

One summer, I learned that it wasn't hard to make a bomb.

Rob had a mother and a father, and he was my best-friend. His father worked. A lot. His mother shuttled Rob's sister to and from gymnastics practices, meets, expos, competitions. A lot. My mom always says that if Rob had been at our house even a millisecond more during the week she probably could have filed him as a dependent on her taxes. Rob ate with us, slept at our house, helped take care of my mom's daycare kids. His big mouth and gangly body feature prominently in many home movies of my childhood.

Rob's dad coached our little league basketball team. Neither of us deserved to start, but we did. For every errant pass out of bounds, for every travelling call, for every double-dribble, we ran gassers. Run up the court, touch the baseline. Run back. Touch the baseline. Run up. Touch. Run, Run. Touch. We were nine years old.

Rob said he'd seen it on TV. I doubted it but went along anyway. Earlier in the spring the backhoes and bobcats chewed up our yard to make space for the pool Mom had promised us for Christmas. The dirt had to go somewhere. And so it did. In huge piles to the left and to the right of the newly flattened land. Our yard sloped significantly, and even though we wanted an aboveground pool, a lot of land needed to be excavated.

For a few weeks running up and down the ten-foot-tall piles seemed fun enough. But then: aluminum foil (rolled into dime-sized balls), an empty two-liter soda bottle rinsed of any residue, cold water, and pellet-form Drano (that I had to steal from Dad's basement the weekend before–dual custody had its benefits). Boom!

The key was not to get caught holding the concoction once mixed. Stories from across the neighborhood of lost fingers and bloodied faces made us nervous, but not nervous enough to stop.

My mom worked in the afternoons and so we were left with a new VHS and some microwave pizza. And way too much dirt.

Step One: dig a hole in the dirt mound big enough to swallow whole the two-liter bottle.

Step Two: roll up twenty–thirty balls of foil and drop them into the empty two-liter.

Step Three: pour in two–three scoops of pellet-form Drano.

Step Four: pour in water until bottle is half-full. Do this step quickly.

Step Five: shake the two-liter vigorously for ten–fifteen seconds.

Step Six: put the bomb in the hole.

Step Last: Run like a motherfucker. Laugh. Repeat.

*

The problem: the stump of a tree recently struck and grounded by a late summer lightning storm. The solution: men and what they don't know. We–my dad, his buddy Doug, and I–in the woods behind Doug's house, stacked three to four foot pieces of the tree we'd just broken down further via chainsaw on its former and now leveled stump. We hacked, with rubber-gripped axes, chunks of the fallen sugar maple into firewood. Doug had called my dad the night before after the storm raged through our Crystal Lake neighborhood, said he needed to borrow the Trailblazer and flatbed trailer. It was Dad's weekend, and so I tagged along, my lanky fifteen-year-old arms, my basketball-fit legs, muscles built for explosion, not for repeated stress, not for manual labor. But I reveled in it. The musk of dying tree, the sweet of maple, of sawdust and men and indecision and "yeah, the Blazer can definitely haul all this." But we didn't know. We didn't know anything. We didn't know anything except that our bodies kept chopping, kept stacking, kept working because it felt good, made us stand taller and take notice of one another through squinted eyes and heavy breaths. What men do, men do together. And we were together.

I didn't know Doug, had only met Doug at cook-outs and

weekend threesomes at Twin Ponds where Dad taught me to *keep my elbow tucked, turn at the hips, extend through the ball* and Doug tagged along; his marriage on the rocks, he had nowhere else to be. He worked in finances. Made deals, broke deals, talked constantly of "seriously, I can get you 2,000% back on this investment. You in?" He had a cell phone before anyone else I knew had one. Two and three times per round he'd answer its ring: "Hell-lllo. Doug here." I never saw him wear sunglasses, but he was obviously sensitive to the sunlight. He scrunched his eyes nearly closed as he guided the chainsaw through the maple, wrinkled his brow in a pose of constant pain and irritation not from physical exertion but from trying to keep the light from his eyes. He never looked comfortable, always looked to be a moment away from bursting into flames if he looked too high across the horizon.

*

My father, when he tried to quit smoking, used to suck on aquarium stones he sterilized at work. He claimed they worked better than candy or gum, which his doctor recommended. He'd slip a stone under his tongue, massage it hard against his gums as if he could somehow suck smoother the smooth stone.

My father and I talked about little else than fishing—I was thirteen, in love with things muscular and flesh-like—and we wished to become night-hunters, gifted with vision known only to owls and walleyes. Our arms would twist into fins, our jaws would crack and lengthen to gills, and our throats would no longer swell with air. We would not swim so far that bait could not reach us. He would not swim so far that I could not reach him.

Days would pass in conversation and then not, and I'd think him dead, the sound of a stone rolling across his teeth imagined. Silence makes noise when silence is all there is. Just a whisper, something louder than an inhale. And I'd drag nets to snag him, cast lines and bait hooks, whip my legs into a tail and swim from shore to bay. I'd find my father there, a bluegill in his mouth – his teeth, cracked and marked from the stones, pushed long and deep into the bluegill's body.

*

It took Dad, Doug, and I six hours to strip the tree with chainsaws from a thirty-foot behemoth to pieces small enough to stand on edge and chop into usable logs. We groaned and swore, threw our weight against the fifty-year-old maple until our fingers blistered and the smalls of our backs cramped with exhaustion. My dad's skin blotched, both reddened and paled beneath a heavy sweat, his forehead a billboard of sunburn and dehydration.

We lined the back of the Trailblazer with old blankets and sheets and stacked rows of the logs floor to ceiling. Next, the flatbed. Doug made piles of three logs – which was about as much as we could carry safely – and Dad and I balanced the bushels across our forearms, hauled them to the trailer, made five columns of ten logs each, three logs high. Over 150 logs of firewood and still some of the tree remained.

"Where are we taking this again?" my dad asked as we took turns with the garden hose, pouring water down our dry throats and across our sunburned necks.

"My cousin has some land just north of the lake," Doug said, his right hand blocking the sun from his face, huge drops of sweat peeling down his left cheek. "Unless you want it? I'm sure he wouldn't mind." Doug brought his axe down against a log, split it in two, and the halves fell to their respective sides of the stump. "I never tire of how that works each and every time."

My dad and I sensed it simultaneously: Doug didn't have a

plan, had nowhere to move the wood. Dad nodded at me to hand him the hose. He took a long drink, let the water run over his face, across his eyes and into his hair. He shook his head and a fine mist of cold water sprayed into the air in front of him.

"Yeah, I could probably use it," my dad said. Still dripping, he picked up three more logs and dropped them onto the flatbed, lined them up with the ones beneath, pushed on them to make sure they were secure, wiped his brow on his shirt sleeve. "Yeah, definitely."

*

Just because we tied perfect knots.

Just because we cut holes in old tires and slipped them over the dock stabilizers to act as fenders.

Just because I practiced and practiced tying a cleat hitch.

Just because we tied perfectly to each hitch arm.

Just because each hitch was newly fastened to the dock.

Just because there was enough slack in each line to let the boat bounce in the wind-whipped lake.

Just because we double-checked each knot.

Just because we braved the torrential rain to bring all our gear from the boat to the basement—anchor, gas can, oars, and piss jug included.

Just because we took our time, didn't hurry, knew better than to worry about staying dry more than protecting the boat, our gear, our next trip to Mielke Bay.

Just because we'd tied to that dock for generations, boats among boats, in storm after storm.

Didn't mean the damn thing wouldn't sink.

Didn't mean we didn't know you couldn't tie the boat nose facing the shore when the water got rough.

Didn't mean we didn't know the weight of the 9.9HP Johnson

outboard would hold the back of the boat under the lake just long enough after each wave crested.

*

Approval or acknowledgement from my father sounds something like a mix between a two year old answering a question of want ("Do you want a cookie?" "Uh-huh") and a scowling, surly parent showing disappointment with a shake of their head, an internal *what will we ever do with you* ("Mm, mm, mm").

"Was it hard being divorced when I was only three?"

"Uhm huhm."

"That's a hell of a song."

"Uhm huhm."

"Holy shit! That car almost hit us! What a jerk!"

"Uhm huhm."

And in my head: "I wish we could talk more about this shit."

"Uhm huhm."

Maybe that was enough? Just being acknowledged. Just being under the umbrella of a man-to-man conversation. Like on Big Arbor Vitae, a cigarette inconceivably balanced on Dad's lips–only physics beyond my comprehension could explain how it didn't fall to the bottom of the boat, extinguish in the spray settled there from our trip from shore to Mielke Bay–the silence around us punctured only by loon calls and badger splashes and "uhm huhms," all answers to questions best kept quiet.

*

Didn't mean we didn't know we could run from Aunt Mary's cabin to the dock in under ten seconds.

Dad and I untied the knots as the rain and waves soaked our

jeans and sweatshirts. The lake, only weeks post-thaw, rocked the boat hard into our tire fenders, and we narrowly escaped with our hands a few times bone-crushing blows as the aluminum jon boat slammed against the dock.

"Untie, untie!" my grandpa yelled from the foot of the dock. There wasn't enough room on the dock for him, too, and he couldn't bend quickly enough to help anyway, so he yelled instead: "It's going to pull the whole damn dock down!" I reversed the knot at the nose of the boat. Back, under, over, through. No. Through, over, under, back. I couldn't remember the sequence. Damn it. Back, over, through, under. Yes. That did it. And then I heard a splash. Dad had jumped into the lake and crawled into the boat, stood, up to his knees in the water, on the middle seat. The water crashed into his waist. He just stood there, didn't know what to do. Then he reached for the plug at the back of the boat, the one we never knew the reason for. But pulling it out did nothing.

"Get me a bucket," he finally said.

"For what?" Grandpa asked.

"We have to start bailing it out."

"Dennis, it's underwater."

Grandpa, bad knees and back and hips and all, walked out on the dock, motioned for me to move over, and reached down to help my dad up, but not before he told him to grab the rope tied to the front of the boat. "We'll pull it out, all three of us, to the shore."

And we did. The damn thing weighed hundreds of pounds, the weight of water never more impressive. Once on the shore, the boat angled nose up, the purpose of the plug became readily apparent. Water poured out the back of the boat as rain continued to come down harder than we'd ever seen. When the water level fell below the motor we were able to disconnect it from its mounting and unplug the fuel line, and when the water level fell below the seats we three were strong enough to tip the boat to its side and then finally over completely. Dad and I carried the motor into the basement, set it on workbench, and stared at it.

"It's waterlogged," I said.

Dad walked around to the other side of the bench. "Uhm huhm."

"Can we fix it?"

Dad played with the pull start, jiggled the steering mechanism, watched the water dripping from the encasement over the motor make puddles on the cold basement floor. "Uhm huhm."

*

On Lake Big Arbor Vitae, in Mielke Bay, in our twelve-foot jon boat, always hot coffee, heavy on the cream and sugar. Always layers: long underwear, sweatpants, jeans. Two pairs of socks, one woolen. A t-shirt, hoodie, jacket, rain jacket, a vest to keep the chest warmest. Gloves, but only until they're too annoying: have you ever tried to unhook a walleye with gloves on? My father's lit cigarette the only light for miles. That orange speck like Daisy's green pier light. Artists know symbolism. I just know my father.

*

Grandpa and Dad spent several hours in the basement the night the boat sank alternately swearing, drinking beer, and tinkering with the motor. A couple times I came down from the warmth of the cabin to check on their progress – I was told to go inside, get warm, eat something. They had a pile of tools – screwdrivers, wrenches, an old hairdryer they used to try to dry the electrical components. Dad would stare at a problem for hours, would try different and various tactics, even if he knew the solution would never materialize. His way didn't include giving up, didn't include surrendering to the fact that some problems don't have solutions. But the motor proved more complex than the crossword and metal ring puzzles he occupied himself with at home, and eventually he and Grandpa snuck upstairs to bed sometime after midnight.

Dad walked to the campgrounds where we rented our boats each spring at the end of the block the next morning while Grandpa and I fried some eggs and bacon. He came back on a golf cart with a new motor, this one a 15 H P Johnson. "This'll get us to Mielke Bay alright!" After breakfast we mounted the new motor and tied the boat to the dock, this time, nose out. We didn't talk about it again. Not that day anyway. But the next year, on our first night at the cabin, I noticed a copy of *Outboard Motors Maintenance and Repair Manual* on the table, and that seemed right. Motors could be fixed. There were manuals for those.

*

We dreamed we were fatherless. Motherless. Less. We dreamed we were astronauts. We dreamed we were architects and lived in houses with no walls, only windows and perches for our pet hawks, aquariums for the piranha we'd catch ourselves one day in the Amazon. We dreamed nomadically. We rode our bikes from Cary to Fox River Grove, from Fox River Grove to Cary, from Cary to Crystal Lake, sometimes all the way to McHenry or Bull Valley. We crossed county lines, squatted in mink farms, hiked through cornfields until we got lost, couldn't orient ourselves, the sun above us hot and directionally useless. We lost ourselves but never each other. We listened: "Have fun, boys. Be safe, and be back for dinner, please." One of us always wore a watch. We fished every pond and backwards lake or stream we could find. Twelve years old. BMX bikes. A backpack full of peanut butter sandwiches, bottles of water or cans of Pepsi, some quarters if we had to call home in an emergency, and fishing gear: lures, hooks, sinkers, knives, pliers, bobbers, measuring tape, disposable cameras, week-old chicken leftovers for the catfish, secured, of course, in airtight Ziploc bags. Each of us also carried two to three rods held cross-wise on our handlebars. We rode carefully. We rode hard. We fished. We sunburned. We dreamed of pike and bass, sunfish and gar, coyotes, snapping turtles, tits and ass. We flirted at the playgrounds found near so many little streams. The girls often ran off, and we'd laugh, nervously, unsure of ourselves or our purposes, and assume we'd get them next time. We had no idea what we'd do if you ever did *get them*. It didn't matter. The three of us riding down the middle of the road took up the whole road. We sauntered. We sweat. We dreamed of fish so large we'd have to empty our packs on the shore just to fit them in, fish so large the girls on the playground might do to us what they would do to us if we caught a fish so large.

*

Mielke Bay again.

"We never did talk about your mom and I."

"I know."

It was 36 degrees that May midnight. Ice formed on the tip of my pole. Between casts I had to break it off. But the walleye were biting.

"Dad?"

"Yeah."

"I'm fucking cold."

*

My father never stops explaining. How rivers work, how playing cards are made, how a fish's weight increases eight-fold every time its length is merely doubled. My father never stops explaining the physical world. How snake jaws unhinge to swallow prey larger than their heads, how zone defense is only as strong as its weakest defender. My father explains that a male lion will ejaculate thirty times a day while mating, but intercourse lasts only seconds each time. A day on Venus is longer than its year. The platypus is poisonous and a mammal. In that story, he is the platypus, Mom is a different mammal, and my sister and I are just babies. It's a common language is facts. Our relationship grows the more we learn about the world.

For years I'd spend every other Saturday trying to sleep on an old pull-out couch in the McGonagles' basement with my sister and the McGonagle kids, Ryan and Molly, while the adults played round after round of Trivial Pursuit. The random facts, the dates of assassinations (Anwar Sadat, President of Egypt, October 6, 1981), the weight of the heaviest ball of twine (Darwin, Minnesota: 17,400 pounds, and it took 42,340 hours to create), the world's deepest unaided free dive (236 feet), the tallest giraffe (19' 11"), how many muscles it takes to smile (12) versus how many muscles it takes to frown (11), though it's a commonly held belief that it takes far less *effort* to smile than to frown.

Eventually they'd drink their way past Trivial Pursuit and start a spirited, if not alcohol-induced, game of Pictionary. In the morning us kids would find drawings of penises (or "grain silos"), tits (or "dinner plates"), buildings, stop signs, silhouettes of lawn chairs and ask what they all meant. My dad, flipping pancakes at the stove, would say, "I don't remember. But it was a good game," and the other adults would laugh.

The written word didn't exist until nearly 5,000 years ago when the Sumerians invented Cuneiform. Before that, a pictographic culture of nonverbal communication sustained long-term storytelling. The printing press, invented in 1454 by Gutenberg, changed the written culture into one no longer relegated to the wealthy and noble. The first cave paintings, found in France, date to 40,000 years ago and feature hand stencils and red etchings of non-bipedal animals – perhaps the hunted or perhaps the hunters. But a penis with arms shaking hands with a waffle, a waffle whose eyes appear rolled back in its head – wait, is that a hand the penis is shaking? – didn't appear in pictographs until Saturdays in the late 1980s when my dad never stopped explaining salinity, how rivers pick up rocks and soil but that once they empty into the ocean, the water evaporates faster than the salt sinks. *Some fish*, he explains, *can move from salt water to fresh water and back. Some fish are simply more adaptable than others.*

CONFESSION

Do prepare to prepare to say something about the color of the leaves. The badger that lives out back. The geography of the place, or the breakfast you shared. Be prepared to talk about the tornado siren that didn't go off in time. The syllabus left at the bus stop, how much you spent on albums from '90s punk bands. Your confession is that you never confessed. Find the last green in the backyard this late winter morning and look through it: pine needles fall off the pine trees and into the second person. Consider this a fair warning. All night you dream of something wet and unstable: your legs kick and your moans gargle. Here's your chance to fix your dreams with talk. Prepare to examine carpet squares that don't match; the room, then, a giant puzzle, one you have to walk through to solve. After three days, and even in water, tulips will hang their heads, and you can't help but feel responsible. Prepare to leave the bedroom window open overnight. It's okay, it won't rain. If I may: I want to be wet with something. You are the hands in my pockets pulled out just in time to balance. Prepare to drink from this.

RHYTHM IS ORIGINALLY THE RHYTHM OF THE FEET

Of birth and death. Movement and lowering into the soil, beyond and then the incorporeal, wraith, the shade of ever. Running as obsession. Running as clarity. The creation of. The absolution in. Threnody. Ode. Palinode. Genethliacon. Elegy. Born and born again. *To celebrate*: much-frequented, kept solemn. Like prayer and thanksgiving. Like the body overcoming.

*

At first I couldn't run at all. Two hundred eighty pounds. Years–fifteen years–of bodily abuse hung on a once-in-shape frame. My shins throbbed, the muscles tensed, and bones stressed after only a quarter mile. The bottoms of my feet cramped and my lungs felt overinflated, heavy with internal sweat or pins and needles or some other river of pain, the threshold far past. The pounding, the force, nearly a thousand pounds of pressure per step–or something equally difficult to conceive of. Tendons, ligaments. My muscles would adapt, slowly. But those other fibers, the less malleable ones, would be forced to burden the load until then. My body couldn't perform the demands I placed on it, couldn't bear my weight or my effort.

*

How and why we move. Migration and purposeful movement versus potential movement and static contractions.

Migration: The white-rumped sandpiper, a shorebird, not much bigger than a sparrow, breeds in habitats above the Arctic Circle. Every fall it migrates to South America to overwinter. Before it embarks on the opening 2,500 mile leg – over two days and nights, nonstop – the sandpipers fatten up. Their bellies full, they fly all the way to Suriname, on South America's north coast. They fatten up again, and then it's 2,200 miles overland across the continent, through the Amazon, and finally to Argentina to complete the 9,000-mile one-way trip from, nearly, pole to pole. At the end of each of their migrations, in the fall and spring, the birds again reach continuous daylight, after having come from the midnight sun. In short, except for when in transit, the world the white-rumped sandpiper experiences is without night.

My journey, my migration, started, like so many of my previous adventures, with reading. I turned to Bernd Heinrich's *Why We Run: A Natural History*. Little did I know the lessons it contained, the wisdom one could garner simply by understanding human locomotion.

Heinrich explains potential movement thusly, "Play serves a vital function in many animals. It serves the ultimate function of practice, and it is motivated by pleasure. Pleasure is a proximate mechanism for achieving many ultimate benefits." And since the mind serves as the mediator between sensory input and physiological output, we know that playing, frolicking, call it what you will, means health, means life, means muscles contract and hearts beat and lungs expand.

*

You fall you fall you fall. It's maic. It's not hard to run. It's actually, given gravity's persistence, impossible not to. Stand in the middle of a room, at the threshold of a driveway or a sidewalk, anywhere. Feet shoulder-width apart. Knees gently flexed. Relax. Now bend. But not at your hips or at your knees or at your waist. Instead, lean forward at the ankles. Lean far enough and let gravity do its job: you fall. Now put a foot down to turn your fall into a step, keep your lean, and stride with the other foot. You're running. You've fallen and you'll keep falling so long as you keep your core tight, your hips relaxed and legs pistoning, your chest forward, head level.

*

Last year, a friend, who just weeks before had nearly died of alcohol poisoning (he had woken up in an ICU, and learned his BAC had been 0.42 when friends brought him to the hospital), texted me to say, "I just ran eight miles in 45 minutes." Jesus. That's a sub-6:00 pace. "Just thought it might feel good to stretch my legs a bit." Granted, he used to be an athlete, had a DI basketball scholarship in his pocket until an illness derailed him. Jealousy: it's not only for artists, ex-lovers, and politicians. I wanted, now at 260 pounds, to run like that, to just forget about *midfoot strike...core tight...relax at the shoulders...swing arms perpendicular and not in front of—*

*

Greece. Pheidippides. Not 26.2 miles but over 140. He ran all day, through the night, into the morning, again through the day, at least. *Running* as a preposition. *Around, through, into.* An Athenian herald, an *hemerodrome*, "day-runner." A professional runner. The Persian forces outside Athens, ready to squash, plunder, pilfer: the hardness of consonants—maybe wars start *here*. The plains of Marathon, the severely outnumbered Athenian army. Send someone, the Athenian generals commanded, to Sparta. So he ran. The Spartans could not fight until the moon was full, so Pheidippides brought that message back to the Athenians – 140 miles, all day and through the night and into the day and night again. He missed a surprise attack: 6,400 Persian bodies lay dead; 192 Athenians. The Persians fled to their ships, hoped to beat the Greeks to Athens, to take their city if they couldn't take their army. Pheidippides. Carry the news, the generals commanded, of our victory and the approaching Persian ships. Two hundred eighty miles, and now a final dash – twenty-six miles – from the plains to the city. The hemerodrome warned Athens and collapsed, died shortly thereafter from exhaustion as the Athenians arrived in town to thwart the Persian's attempt on the city.

*

The first recorded account of the word *joy*: a word of greeting uttered when Pheidippides announced Athenian victory. Lucian tells us this in *Pro lapsu inter salutandum.* "Joy to you, we've won! Joy to you." And then, death from exhaustion.

From the Greek: *Nikomen*: "We have won." *Chairtei*: "Hail!"

From Robert Browning's "Pheidippides":

So, when Persia was dust, all cried "To Akropolis!
Run, Pheidippides, one race more! the meed is thy due!
'Athens is saved, thank Pan,' go shout!" He flung down his shield,
Ran like fire once more: and space 'twixt the Fennel-field
And Athens was stubble again, a field which a fire runs through,
Till in he broke: "Rejoice, we conquer!" Like wine through clay,
Joy in his blood bursting his heart, he died – the bliss!

Pheidippides met the god Pan, halfway to Sparta, above Tegea on Mount Parthenion. Pan promised him protection, glory, faith, as long as his message was successful, and he agreed to fight against the Persians, for in addition to his other powers, Pan was known for his capacity to instill an extreme sort of fear, an irrational, blind fear, one that could freeze the mind and destroy any sense of judgment—panic. *Panic*: a fear which dominates and prevents reason. Did Pheidippides really meet Pan? Was it a delusion brought on by exhaustion? Surely he believed in the gods, felt their presence often. I once read William Ralph Inge: "To become a popular religion, it is only necessary for a superstition to enslave a philosophy." Was Pheidippides delusional? In order for a vision to be called a delusion, it must meet three criteria: 1) certainty, 2) incorrigibility, and 3) impossibility. But if the vision involves a value judgment (i.e., the belief that gods are, or are not, real and visible), then it's not a delusion because it can never be proven untrue.

*

Pheidippides ran 26 miles on that last jaunt from the plains to the city, but the modern marathon is 26.2 miles because the Queen of England wanted the runners to finish in front of her seats at the Olympic Stadium, which was 385 yards from the original 26-mile finish line.

*

Muscles are one of those things most of us take for granted. They are the engines of our bodies—they turn energy into motion. It is impossible to do anything without muscles: express an idea, run, build. Eat. Fuck. Skeletal muscles we can see; smooth muscles push blood, food, sperm, and egg; cardiac muscles stretch barely but contract forcefully, involuntarily. Twitch, twitch. Skeletal muscles always come in pairs: the pectorals pull your arms to your front side; lats pull your arms to your back. *For every action, there is an equal and opposite reaction.* A sustained contraction: power: tetanus. You think it and they move: voluntary. We're used to the libidinal force of blood, the swooning, the pumping, the sweating, and sometimes it's used to us, too: the differences between *faith of feeling* and *faith of event*: one is voluntary, one is involuntary. Or vice versa.

At 250 pounds, ligaments have stretched a bit. Soreness occurs, but as my training journal attests, "the pain, the searing-awful-can't-walk pain, is lessening and I can breathe and enjoy this, finally." I'm still only running two miles at a time, often taking well over twenty-five minutes to do it, but my legs feel full, strong, less like rubber bands and more like cables.

I didn't yet have it in my head – I wasn't a *runner* – but I had it in my legs.

*

The communal chase is part of our biological makeup. We're hungry? We hunt. To hunt? We run, we chase. We want to mate? We display physical prowess. To do so, we jump or lift or hunt, and to hunt, we run.

To run we churn. Together and alone, in loud packs and in solitary quiet. We know, evolutionarily, that over great distances, no animal can outrun us. Think of a car, its gas tank full. Without our intervention, it can only go, perhaps, several hundred miles. Though over a short distance, say a quarter mile, that same car could reach speeds of 125 miles per hour and complete its journey in twelve seconds. We do not move quickly as well as a car, but with minimal nutrition – think plants and fruit found along our journey, on the side of trails, in deserts, in forests, on the shores of rivers, lakes, streams—we can run for thousands of miles, day after day after day until we find what it is for which we yearn.

What we have that other animals, that machinery, do not is an enduring desire to be nowhere and everywhere at once.

*

Heinrich writes, "Movement is almost synonymous with life. With elongating stems and twirling tendrils, plants race one another toward light." Likewise, seeds compete to be first—in the wind, in a migrating bird's stomach (to be dropped later, of course), in the river, and, finally, in the ground. But plants and seeds aren't conscious, don't move *voluntarily*.

Humans harness chemistry and propel, through the power of our mind/muscle connection (an instantaneous synaptic mechanism), ourselves forward, backward, in any plane of motion—even upward and over vast distances, as we have not only harnessed our bipedal muscles but also our brains: we control, now, motion through the air, through water, over land, at speed. We have built machinery to do our locomotion for us.

But how far, and how hard, can we push ourselves? There's research about cortisol production when the body becomes overexerted due to exercise; the muscles break down too far, lose too much oxygen and blood to be rebuilt, and at that point, exercise is counterproductive. This is why we train, why we increase the distances we can run, slowly and over time. We teach our bodies to deal with stress, physiological, psychological, hormonal. We have to *condition* ourselves. We *could* give up, we probably *should* stop before exertion. By definition, as Heinrich points out, "Stress is the expenditure of energy. [We] can't *live* without it."

At 220 pounds, I could finally match the effort with the results. Heinrich, my touchstone, my witness, writes about how in bipedal animals there happens a decoupling between breathing and the runner's gait. Essentially, he says that the energy we use to run cannot also simultaneously be used to ventilate the lungs. It's a conundrum our biology can't overcome. Ideally, though, the runner should couple her arm swings with her stride and her stride with her breathing. Left arm, right leg, inhale; right arm, left leg, exhale. Repeat. Contrary to the decoupling, we can maintain an equilibrium between effort and pace, pace and our desire to get stronger. I sweat just as hard, but I started to enjoy it, the effort, the process, the exertion. I looked forward to each outing, and missed it when parenthood and work wouldn't allow me the time to run. My body started to change. Muscles lengthened and strengthened, fat melted, and my heart knew now to expect the extra work. *Became accustomed.*

It's not exactly the theory of progressive load increments, but it's like that. The theory has been known and employed since ancient times. According to Greek mythology, Milo of Croton, wanted, in his early teen years, to be the strongest man the world had ever seen and embarked upon this mission by lifting and carrying a calf every day. As the calf grew and became heavier, Milo became stronger. Finally, when the calf had developed into a full-grown ox, Milo, thanks to the long-term progression, was able to lift the ox. He was the strongest man in the world.

I wanted to be the fastest runner I could be and so I ran farther and harder, making time when I had no time, and with the constant thought, as Heinrich writes, "In evolution, almost every solution is the result of compromises."

*

Science tells us that the basic molecular processes are the same in all three types of muscle fibers. Striate appears as alternating stripes of light and dark when viewed under polarized light. You think about moving your arm and your nervous system fires: contract! It reminds me of Edmund Burke's writing on the sublime: "It is our ignorance of things that causes all our admiration, and chiefly excites our passions." During contraction, thin fiber slides against thick fiber and each shortens, creating bridges, proteinic filaments stronger in numbers than when alone. The muscle shortens and produces force: energy into motion into strength into capacity.

An essay in which everything is a metaphor for everything else, except *everything* is the way the body works and *everything else* is also the way the body works.

*

The debate between heel strikers and midfoot strikers continues in the running world. Who is less likely to get injured? Which is better for the body? Which is the more normal, ancestral approach to running? But at two hundred pounds, I started to gain confidence in the midfoot strike, in the less percussive pounding, in the natural forward lean necessary to achieve such a movement. My calves ached less, my core became stronger, and I could run, more or less, as far as the calorie surplus I'd created would last.

There's always, though, a give and take. Yes, I could run for as long as my body metabolized and fueled itself, but that system is, like the body as a whole, flawed. Energy, like time, is inherently slippery. Heinrich – O Captain! my Captain!:

All of the bipedal animals that run fast do so by a rapid succession of long leaps, either alternating between legs or kicking off with both legs at the same time. There is considerable heavy impact of the feet striking the ground, and with that impact comes a potential loss of energy. However, mechanisms have evolved to harness some of this otherwise wasted energy. It's in the anatomy. As the foot is depressed on landing, the heel (Achilles') tendon is stretched, and when the foot rebounds with liftoff on the toes, the just-stretched tendon, or springing ligament, contracts and releases stored energy.

So it makes sense to initiate that coiling as effectively and safely as possible. Hence the midfoot strike.

The sublimity of force, of *gait*, of contract and stretch and stretch and contract, and how often animals' gaits have rhythm. Heard together, rich and hoofed, they become herds of drummers.

The sublime as a pleasing fear. If I just keep running. If I run *that* far from home, will I be able to run all the way back? As Burke writes about in *A Philosophical Enquiry into the Origin of Our Ideas of the Sublime and Beautiful*, the sublime can be seen as the fantastic realization of terror transformed into pleasurable horror, elegant awfulness. *Ecstasy* isn't the right word, and neither is *freeing*. The clichéd nature of running away from your problems, or hitting the road to stop the mind from its turning exist because, like most clichés, they're true. But what I felt as I learned to run from within and from without.... It's strange, the impulse to run when you're not chasing something.

People ask me all the time: Why do you run? Why not just eat less and do more moderate exercise, like a stationary bike or something, instead of stressing your body so much? "Stress is the expenditure of energy. [W]e can't live without it." We already know this. And besides, people do some rather bizarre things to 1) satisfy their curiosity, 2) pique their interest in things different from themselves, and/or 3) to test themselves against either odds or others. Heinrich tells this story of a friend who did all three of those simultaneously. He writes of a colleague at the University of California who "chase[d] lizards on a miniature racetrack until they could go no farther. Then he grabbed them and ground them up in a blender." In doing so, he could measure their lactic acid generation. "By assaying lizards after varying sprint durations, and at varying postsprint intervals, he was able to determine that it takes some lizards an hour or more to get rid of their lactic acid load."

This urge to run, or grind up lizards to study exercise physiology, comes down to, perhaps, one trait all humans share: what you have is less important than what you do with it. This simple fact allows us to keep reaching, which then allows us achievement, and achievement is what sometimes defines us.

*

Evolution isn't fair. Neither is the process it takes to change oneself. Heinrich tells us the incredible story that takes place in the relatively harsh winter of 1985–86, three-quarters of South Dakota's fifty thousand pronghorn antelope died "from cold, heavy snow, and wind. And fences." Not able to escape the brutal weather, the ruminants piled up behind fences and died. Pronghorn antelope are one of nature's freaks: they can jump astonishingly far, but they have not evolved the ability, like their forest-dwelling cousins, the white-tailed deer, to make vertical leaps. For the muscles packed in their legs, the task should be trivial, but its mind doesn't make the connection. Again, "The mind leads, the body follows. A pronghorn antelope can't conceive of jumping over a fence."

*

April 14, 2013: The doctor calls to tell me that my HBA1C is 12.8%. In other words, I am a thirty-three-year-old type 2 diabetic. Fuck that. On April 15, I ran.

Scientists used to think that our ability to run was simply a by-product of our bipedalism, of our ability to walk, that because we could walk we naturally, evolutionarily, just one day decided to pick up the pace and run. In a 2004 study published *Nature*, University of Utah biologist Dennis Bramble and Harvard University anthropologist Daniel Lieberman dispute that argument and posit that modern humans evolved from apelike ancestors because they *needed* to run long distances, perhaps to hunt or scavenge on the vast African savannas. It wasn't because we *could* but because we *had to*. Those vultures on the horizon, certainly circling over a recently dead animal—our dinner!—are an hour walk away, but if I run I could be there in twenty minutes and eat and feed my family. This ability, they conclude, could have shaped our anatomy, and not the other way around. Our tendons became springlike, our ligaments, too. Our toes shortened to help us create downward force to push forward, and our shoulders evolved to rotate independently of our heads and necks to allow us better balance. Running made us human—at least in an anatomical sense. The emergence of the Homo species is tied directly to the evolution of running.

Humans, compared to other running animals, are poor sprinters, but we are, again comparatively, adept at running long distances. We evolved endurance, not speed; hunters and gatherers needed to balance caloric expenditure with potential caloric intake, and we all know that slow and steady.... Heinrich tells us, "Speed is meaningless unless the distance is specified." I've always thought that even the basest of animals knows that scavenging is a more reliable source of food than hunting, but to scavenge well, one has to either be at the right spot at the right time or get to the right spot quickly.

September 15, 2013: The doctor calls to tell me that my HBA1C is 4.6% (between 4.5 and 6.0 is normal). In other words, I am a healthy thirty-three-year-old. Because I ran. But I wouldn't stop running. It wasn't a sprint; I wouldn't outrun what was inevitable, what was chasing me – death chases all of us, and none of us can outrun it – but I could endure the process, and enjoy it.

Running, though, is hard work. Just because we've evolved to do it, doesn't mean it's easy. We have to train, our bodies and minds. Training involves not only the physiological adaptation of the muscle fibers, but also the neurological coordination in recruiting them to do their work. But when the brain and legs work together, the hard work becomes, at least, less noticeable.

Heinrich again, helps me understand, when he writes, "At the most efficient running stride, arms, breaths, and heartbeats are multiples of one another. Those multiples change with pace and effort, but the synchronicity does not. It is as though his legs beat the tune to create the body's rhythm." But our pace and stride and breath change depending on strategy, on tactics, on our competitors. They are impacted by our meals, our goals. And our *progress.*

I can't say it better than Heinrich. At our best, "the distance runner must fairly float along the ground."

*

I haven't evolved. Except that I have. Running, unlike lifting weights, requires relatively little restructuring of the body. Given proper nutrition and gravity, our bodies know how to fall one foot at a time. The only question then is, What's your motivation? D.H. Lawrence wrote, in *The White Peacock*, "Be a good animal, true to your animal instincts." My instinct? To not be ill, to live a healthy, long life. My friend's instinct after nearly dying of alcohol poisoning? To prove his body still worked, hard, and at his command.

It's not just an escape or a way to trim the waistline – though both of those are damned good reasons to run. For centuries runners have been prized members of their societies. Heinrich tells of the Penobscot tribe in Maine. Each family group had designated runners who would chase down moose and deer – this was considered an honorable position in their culture. The provider. The caretaker. The hunter. The runners, though, were guarded by old men, as Heinrich writes, "to make sure they did not have sex, that they slept with their legs drawn up, and that they didn't chew spruce gum, as those transgressions were thought to impair their breathing as well as make their testicles clack when they ran, warning the deer."

Humans no longer need to run – to eat, to survive, to escape, to scavenge – but our bodies still crave it, the forward falling, the momentum, the exertion, the lung-heart, the bellows-pump. Our blood is designed to help us exert; our mitochondrial power (the batteries of our cells that create the energy, used to contract our muscles) has evolved to feed us as we run. We take breaths, complicated structures of silent syntax, like an em dash. Heinrich writes, "We produce blood *to the extent that the body demands*." We can run, theoretically, forever.

*

Finally, 180 pounds. My goal. What I've been running toward, *why* I've been running toward. And away. From. To. I didn't get there via magic but through hard work, through training. Heinrich, all along and even now, understands this magic: "There is a truth, a beauty, and a symmetry in this that is inviolate. Every step counts. Each is an act of beauty. Together they create *stride*, and in terms of the whole, *pace*." I've learned to *pace* myself, to make of determination long-term results.

I've been having this recurring dream. My son and daughter, just five and three, are in a rowboat. There's an oar in the water and one in the hull; the water's dark–midnight green, or rifle almost–and I see them trying to push the one oar, straining their hips, balls of their feet, shoulders and lats, their hands. But they can't move the rowboat–they're stuck in the middle of the pond. Their repeated efforts remind me, inside the dream, of a pendulum swinging perpetually: the speed, the consistency of arc–and the reflections on the surface of the water lift over their heads, this pendulum, one edge of light bumping up against another and starting a different shape–the abstraction of weightlessness. In this dream, my kids are helpless, and every time I wake up sweating, my legs spinning, and my wife says to me, "You're running in your sleep again."

BRICKS BY TYPE

Legos as metaphor. Pathos, too. Especially the giant tub of 1,500 pieces, all colors, all shapes, all types: wheels, worm gears, pulleys, axles, red, orange, blue, mini-figs, claws, eyes, squares, four-dot, six-er. A nomenclature without pretense. A language we shared. A language we could speak in place of the other language we didn't yet need: Ethos. Eric and I. Dad and I. Different weekends, different homes, shared lexicon, common attachments. Pirate ships and dragsters. Sometimes we'd lose pieces. The dogs would find them, the vacuum would find them, our bare feet at midnight would find them as we snuck sleepily to the dark kitchen for a drink of milk. The fact that we got thirsty in the middle of the night was not an act of the imagination, but when we finished rubbing the pain from the arches of our feet and sat down to build something new from disparate blocks, that thirst served its purpose. We awoke from our slumber so we could build both our bodies and something outside ourselves from the thirst inside ourselves. We built in the middle of the night, quietly, with intensity and focus, outside rage or guilt or shame, inside a mirror we couldn't touch.

LYRICISM OF THE FACT: AN ARCHIVE

Every human being, according to some scientists, is living at least eighty milliseconds in the past. Our consciousness lags behind actual events and when we perceive them occurring. Everything has already happened.

The dust in space, because of its chemical makeup, tastes like raspberries.

Early radar echoes of flying birds or unknown sources were referred to as *angels*.

Chemistry is weirder than fiction.

Romans thought giraffes were hybrids between camels and leopards.

A magic potion or charm thought to arouse sexual love, especially toward a specific person, is known as a *philter*.

An elephant will purposefully erect his penis, which is often five feet long, and use it as support when trying to reach food at a tough angle.

If you could magnify an apple to the size of the Earth, the atoms in the original apple would each be about the size of an apple.

Statistically, UFO sightings are at their greatest number during those times when Mars is closest to the Earth.

During WWII, bakers in the US were ordered to stop selling sliced bread on January 18, 1943. Only whole loaves were made available to the public. It was never explained how this action helped the war effort.

Leonardo da Vinci could write with one hand and draw with the other simultaneously.

[Sit me down where love was last. But who will put me there? Who will put me there with eyes?]

BOTH THE BLADE AND THE HANDLE

Magic becomes art when it has nothing to hide.
— BEN OKRI

I am not going to teach you how to make someone disappear.

I *could* teach you how to make someone disappear.

The magician stuffs the silk into his empty hand and when he opens his empty hand it is empty. Remember?

I've started this twice. The first time, I started here: A book about magic should be a book about the eyes. A book about anything should be a book about the eyes. A book about the eyes should be a book about the eyes.

Magic happens everywhere, in every landscape, every earscape.

In poetry: *I will crush lumber / with my teeth* (T.J. Jarrett).

In poetry: *If the water says I'm rain, / listen and believe it* (I don't know).

In thought: *My name means* sober *in sleight-of-hand, means* sleight-of-hand *in drunk.*

In exchanges with four-year-old sons: "Daddy, what's it called when you're really tired at the end of the day?" "Exhaustion?" "No, Daddy, it's called *Let's play a game of checkers.*"

When you look through a window into a dark night—say you're sipping coffee at the dining room table, talking with family, maybe post-Thanksgiving feast, and you turn during a lull to see if it's snowing, but of course it's not—you can see your hazy image reflected in the glass *and* superimposed on the setting just outside. You are staring at yourself staring at yourself.

That is one way you can make someone disappear.

*

In third grade, I saw a magician perform in the school lunchroom. *Assembly*: a group of people gathered together in one place for a common purpose. The magician performed the usual tricks: pull a rabbit from a top hat, levitate a teacher on a plank board previously suspended between two saw horses, change a gallon of water into soda, juice, milk, coffee, and water again. And then, the silk. A yard squared. Red, fantastically red. A soft concerto—or maybe a rock ballad, memory is fuzzy here—blared from the overhead speaker system as he elegantly pushed the silk into his closed fist an inch at a time. A wave or two of the magic wand and his fist, opened triumphantly, was empty.

I made my mom drive me to Ben Franklin. Wal-Mart. K-Mart. Jo-Ann Fabrics. Anywhere I could think of that might sell this vanishing silk. I had to have it. But none of them stocked it. "Maybe it's not sold at a store like ours," they'd say. But then what kind of store might sell it?

This was my introduction to magic. This was my introduction to what's possible.

*

Nothing is impossible. Except maybe something being able to travel faster than the speed of light—though there's an exception here, too: the expansion of the universe microseconds after the

Big Bang when, according to physicist Dr. Michio Kaku, space expanded faster than 186,000 miles per second. But because empty space has zero mass, the Mass-Energy Paradox (i.e. an item's mass increases the faster it moves – think of the way a racecar hugs the track at two-hundred miles per hour: downward force, gravity, the muscle it takes to turn the wheels on a flat course) doesn't apply, but for any other object, because it has mass and therefore must abide by Einstein's relativistic predictions, achieving near light speed, its mass would become infinite and thus no amount of force could any longer propel it at such a speed.

(Though we then have faster-than-light quantum entanglement: subatomic particles can react to information about one another instantly, even if they are separated by vast distances.)

(*Think of any card? Got it? Okay, concentrate on that card, mull it over in your head, turn it upside down on the table, but keep a picture of it in your mind's eye. Concentrate. Okay, I got it. I know your card. Or at least I've narrowed it down to two...*

Ace of Spades.

Queen of Hearts.)

Think of the possibilities?

Quantum particles communicating across continents instantaneously. According to relativity theory, an object moving at the speed of light does not experience the passage of time. Time, essentially, stops. Think of a carousel rotating at light speed. Now imagine yourself on that carousel. Look out at your surroundings. Days will go by in seconds and you will live to thousands of years old while everyone watching you blur by as fast as stars explode, will die, turn to dust, and blow away. You have just time traveled.

∗

Maybe Ponce de León should have looked to the sea rather than to the land. Alchemists should have left behind base metals iń favor of sea-dwelling invertebrates. In Shirahama, Japan, Professor Shin Kubota at Kyoto University's Seto Marine Biological Laboratory has found an animal that doesn't die...exactly. It rejuvenates. The scarlet jellyfish: 4mm by 5mm, a tiny animal, but one with a mysterious ability.

One day in my plankton net—a microscopic animal, real-ly—*there was a small scarlet jellyfish, which had many sharp sticks stuck in its body.... I removed all of the sticks, hoping it may become better and swim again. But it didn't and shrunk.* And then, well, and then.

When a scarlet jellyfish is injured, it goes to the bottom of the ocean floor and morphs back into a polyp, its infant state. Then the polyp, in true Fountain of Youth style, becomes a brand new scarlet jellyfish, moving between an adult and death and back to infant state in about two months. It's the difference between a *trick* and an *illusion*. Tricks communicate little and are inherently meaningless, but with imagination they may be instilled with meaning.

Dr. Kubota has made one specimen rejuvenate an incredible 12 times in his laboratory. *Genetically speaking*, says Dr. Kubota, *jellyfish and humans aren't so different.* And so begins the countdown to human rejuvenation, to immortality, to being born and aging and being born again.

*

Science—in other words, repeated experiments in the field: literally walking up to hundreds of people, black and white, young and old, hip and not—tells me that 51% of the time, male-identifying humans will select, when told to think, quickly, of any one card from an imaginary deck, the Ace of Spades. 52% of female-identifying humans will select the Queen of Hearts. Don't blame me.

*

In college, I paid my bills by performing close-up, walk-around magic at local restaurants, parties, soirées, get-togethers, alcohol-fueled events. With close-up magic, I loved the challenge of maintaining a variety of relationships with several people at the same time. It's not like a big-scale illusion show where you perform for hundreds or thousands of people all in the same position, all with the same relative relationship to the performance: eyes forward, heads titled, leering at the stage props, the assistants, you. And they think collectively: *fool me now, asshole. I see you.* With close-up magic, you manipulate not only the cards, coins, silks, etc, but also your audience's eyes, attention, purpose, posture, and resolve. Close-up magic is the art of misdirection. You need to control the environment. Where people look and for how long. What they see, what they don't see, what they can't see. Angles. Viewpoints.

I'd carry an old camera bag my dad had used, in the late '70s, before I came along, for his Pentax k2, his, as he joked, *firstborn.* In the bag: three decks of cards. One red-backed Bicycle deck, one blue-backed Bicycle deck (depending on the lighting, each color has its benefits and drawbacks), and one blue-backed Bicycle Invisible deck; a set of red sponge balls; Greg Wilson's Dishonest Abe; and four (or five, depending) 1976 bicentennial silver dollars, the best because they had distinctive designs and made for easy misdirection.

I always opened with a card trick, always closed with a coin trick. Well, not *a* coin trick, but *the* coin trick: Shadow Coins. And I learned it – or created my own variation anyway – through trial and error after David Copperfield fooled me – no, *fooled* isn't strong enough a verb. Maybe he *vanquished* me or *flabbergasted* me or *hoodwinked* me—with it on the floor of a Chicago-area diner. Not only did he misdirect, he banished all notions of conceivable explanation. He performed *real* magic.

David Copperfield created his first television special at nineteen years old: *The Magic of ABC Starring David Copperfield*. Donny and Marie, Penny Marshall, Howard Cosell, Abe Vigoda, Cindy Williams, and others, were the special guests. The following year, Orson Welles was the special guest host. Copperfield went on to record nineteen more TV specials—the symmetry of those numbers does not, of course, escape me. David Copperfield owns an island. He dated supermodels, made people disappear from stage to an island halfway across the globe, walked through the Wall of China, survived a tornado of fire, and escaped from Alcatraz. But none of those illusions involved four silver dollars, a square of diner floor carpet, five magic aficionados, and a post-pancake bloat.

I ended up at this diner with Copperfield—as well as my college roommate Raj, one of Copperfield's team members (and underground sleight-of-hand legend and guru) Chris Kenner, and a woman whose name I still don't remember—after getting to meet Copperfield backstage after the Saturday night show at the Allstate Arena. Raj and I simply walked to the front of the stage after the performance, said we knew Kenner from an online chat room (which was a lie) and he'd invited us to meet David. We met Kenner first but didn't mention how we knew him. We fell into an easy conversation and boom, there was Copperfield. We shook hands. I mumbled about idolatry, his flying illusion, *please sign this Ace of Diamonds?* I don't remember getting in a car, driving to the diner, ordering pancakes, eating pancakes, or even how we ended up in the position to tag along.

Traditionally, the Shadow Coins effect—the magician places

four quarters, or other silver coins, at the corners of an imaginary square and seemingly makes them, one at a time, by waving his hands above them, disappear and reappear together and apart in different corners – can be performed in seven, concise, visual steps. Anyone, with a little patience, some knowledge of basic misdirection, and a liter or two of chutzpah could both perform and fool people with the original method of this illusion. But Copperfield's hands merely floated over the coins; he never came within six inches of touching them, and yet still they moved invisibly, teleported, shifted, illusioned. Never had I seen anything like it. I still haven't. He couldn't have had extra coins because his hands never got close enough to the ground to utilize them. He couldn't have used magnets because his hands never got close enough to the ground to utilize them. He made shadows do his dancing. He made the coins – *willed* them to – move from corner to corner. I remember no fast movements. Everything, from the wave of his fingers to the hitch and bend in his wrists, was controlled, slow, mimetic of exactly what we witnessed: the shadows he cast moved the coins. There was no sleight-of-hand; there were no *hands*; just grace and guts. When he was done, we sat there in the booth and nodded. There was nothing to say, nothing to do, nothing.

*

Shadow Coins

1. Begin by placing four quarters on a table to form a square – one at each corner.

Corner 1 = Top Left, Corner 2 = Top Right, Corner 3 = Bottom Left and Corner 4 = Bottom Right.

2. Cup a fifth quarter in your right palm, hidden from view. It is essential that nobody sees this quarter.

3. Slide your right hand over Corner 1 and keep your left hand at Corner 4. You are going to leave the extra quarter at Corner 1 and cup the quarter at Corner 4.

When this is done you will have 2 quarters at Corner 1, 1 at Corner 2 and 1 at Corner 3, with the quarter at Corner 4 missing.

4. Repeat Step #3 with Corner 2. You will be leaving the extra quarter at Corner 2 and sliding away the quarter at Corner 1.

Now you will have 1 quarter at Corner 1, 2 at Corner 2 and 1 at Corner 3.

5. Repeat with Corner 3. You will leave the extra quarter at Corner 3 and slide away the quarter at Corner 2.

This will leave you with 1 quarter at Corner 1, 1 at Corner 2 and 2 at Corner 3.

6. This time, leave the extra quarter at Corner 3 while sliding away the quarter at Corner 1.

This will cause you to have 3 quarters at Corner 3 and 1 quarter at Corner 2. Corners 1 and 4 will be empty.

7. To complete the trick, leave the extra quarter at Corner 3 and slide away the quarter at Corner 2.

A magician never reveals his secrets.

*

When I'm stuck in traffic, I make patterns of the letters and numbers on the license plate in front of me. J216 53K. Okay, I've got 1, 2, 3, 5 and 6. But you can get 4 by subtracting 2 from 6 or by adding 1 and 3. You can get 7 by adding 6 and 1. 8 happens when 5 is added to 3. $9 = 6 + 3$ or $9 = 3 + 5 + 1$. J is the tenth letter of the alphabet. And K is…. Right? Patterns, in nature, are natural – some might say they are at the root of all creation – but patterns in random numbers and letters, that's a condition of the seeker.

Visible regularities of form found in the natural world. This is how the Wikipedia entry on "Patterns in nature" defines its namesake. The natural patterns, which recur in different contexts and are often modelled mathematically, include *trees, spirals, meanders, waves, foams, arrays, cracks and stripes.* We've probably heard of Pythagoras and Fibonacci: $a^2 + b^2 = c^2$ and $F_n = F_{n-1} + F_{n-2}$, …. Many of the patterns we witness in nature are the result of natural selection, but what about some of the more uncanny patterns?

Say I see this on the license plate in front of me: G118 25M. What do I immediately do? I start adding the numbers in my head, trying to make 1–10. And, of course, I can using only two numbers at any one time. In this game, that counts as a victory. But if traffic is really backed up and I put more thought into this, I see my name. G. 1 = A. 18 = R. 25 = Y.M. This can't be an accident, a fluke, a *happenstance.* And I have seen this exact plate. Twice. Years apart. In two different states. Tell me there's no such thing as magic.

Plato argued for the existence of universals; one such universal: the presence of ideal forms. *Physical objects are never more than imperfect copies of these ideal forms.* A tree leaf may well be triangular but it is never a perfect mathematical triangle.

Doesn't this, however, leave room for that most unwelcomed of guests, coincidence? Mathematics governs what patterns can, within any living organism, physically form. Math as an art not a science. *Mathematics*, a teacher once told me, *seeks to discover and explain.* So logarithms and fractals and spirals: these are theories, and theories have laws—but the discovery of those laws come about through creative trial and error.

For instance: *symmetry is pervasive in living things.* Snow-flakes, while each individual in design, always hold to a six-fold symmetry. Crystals are similar; they have either cubic or octahedral symmetries. And then there's rotational symmetry like the rings of Saturn or the ripples formed in a puddle when you drop your keys. The causes of such symmetries are varied and numerous, but expectations, from biological and scientific perspectives, favor the naturally selected, the preordained, the organized.

Trees aim to arrange their leaves as far apart as possible as it maximizes their access to resources.

An idle mind. A combination of letters and numbers. Next time I'm in traffic.

*

As kids we used to explore this neighborhood of run-down and abandoned homes behind the mink farm; we'd walk around, squat, share beers stolen from stepfathers' fridges, ride our BMX bikes, makeout with our girlfriends. One home in particular—a three bedroom, two-story raised ranch, with a tree growing in the foyer—occupied our imaginations most. The oak (at least that's what I remember it being; it could just as easily have been a maple, a beech, something else entirely) had, through some miracle of nature—or purposeful and destructive human intent?–taken root beneath the floor boards and split them from seedling to sapling to almost-mature. The foyer featured a skylight, with the windows long since blown out by storm or thrown stones, above the front door, which provided both sunlight and rainwater. Birds sat on the branches which, through the insulation and warmth of the home, even in the deepest weeks of winter, never fully lost their leaves. Squirrels, however, never had the courage to venture in, though they'd sit atop the skylight's overhang and watch us suspiciously.

Nothing much ever happened there, though I know just sitting beneath that tree became its own ritual, one of *ghosts on a stage*: we often sat quietly thinking, perhaps, of the miracle we sat beneath without being able, or wanting, to articulate its importance. The English landscape painter John Constable once insisted that his art *pleases by reminding, not by deceiving*, and that makes perfect sense. We occasionally wondered aloud how the tree got there, but the subject quickly returned to sports or girls or BMX. The mystery of it satisfied us thoroughly and an explanation would have ruined it.

Magicians guard an empty safe in much the same way. In fact, just like the tree taking root in an old home where the foundation cracked and exposed the floorboards to the soil, there are few secrets that magicians possess that are beyond the capacity of a high-school science class, little technology more complex than a rubber band, a square of mirrored glass, or a length of very thin thread. We overlook too often the simple explanations. The truth is that seldom do the crude gimmicks in a magic show–or in nature–those mirrors, threads, or rubber bands–deceive people. The audience, instead, is taken by the hand and led to deceive themselves.

*

I once wrote a poem about magic.

Once I met a man with only three fingers
on his right hand.

I tried, in fact, for years to write that poem. There's something about magic, about my experience with it: I find it near impossible to manipulate it into language. I'd start with sleights: back palm, tenkai palm, split fan, French drop, retention vanish, Charlier cut, snap change, Elmsley count, Faro shuffle, mechanic's grip. All of it so damn delicious but ultimately useless, meaningless,

Art using Nature for an instrument.

Then I'd try to name names: Horace Goldin, Harry Kellar, John Nevil Maskelyn, Jean Eugène Robert-Houdin, Howard Thurston. But I'd end up where I started:

All the doings of fraudulent persons,
All of it seemed inconsequential –
who, by quickness of movement, or by shadow.

I read theory and practiced, tried to fool myself in the mirror over and again. Sometimes I'd succeed, or maybe I would blink at the exact moment the magic occurred. At my fingertips. Magic: an effect and a method. How we reveal.

He can manipulate coins, lemons, candles
and faith, your wife and vacuums:
an illusion, a plot against the hour,

I needed to understand, first, the senses, how our bodies perceive what our eyes, ears, hands receive. Sense assigned in retrospect: are leaves red because science says leaves will turn red, or does science say they will turn red because they do turn red? In restaurants night after night – The Lighthouse and Applebee's and Stone Creek Inn – I'd place a half-dollar coin in my left palm and close my fingers around it. When I next opened my hand, the coin would have vanished. When a magician places a coin in his hand and makes it disappear – French drop into finger palm into retention vanish–it is a reminder that there's something about coins that we've failed to appreciate. Unlike a mere deception or a simple secret–which most sleight-of-hand is–which gives the impression that something's been taken away, a great magician always makes you feel like something's been given to you.

and sometimes it's best just to forget who you are.

Other times it's best just to forget who you are–

I've forgotten who you are:

From *Magic in Theory* by Lamont: "A definition of misdirection, therefore, should relate to the effect as well as the method. Misdirection may be defined quite simply as 'that which directs the audience towards the effect and away from the method'." In other words, the method and the effect must be separated in time and space.

Dusk now comes, dusk, dusk like a lampshade.

We are told not to have: possession, undress, different state of:

One time I made a freely chosen, signed playing card appear folded in a lemon chosen at random from the bed of lettuce around the salad bar at Stone Creek. The woman who signed the card, who picked the lemon, who cut the lemon in half with her steak knife, screamed at me, "No way!" and punched me, hard, in the shoulder. It spooked me and I dropped the "apparatus," but she was so caught up in the aftermath of *illusion* that she, nor her friends, noticed.

the same plane and strangeness. Implausibilities are the worst

of all nightmares. Out the front window, a diesel downshifts–

It's a case, most times, of one plus one equaling two; more precisely, the hand that I tell you is empty plus the motion of showing it apparently empty and at ease equals your brain telling you the hand is empty. That notion, however, is an illusion. One plus one equals one because I am already one–or two or three or four–steps ahead of you. My hand appears empty but is not. Jim Steinmeyer in *Hiding the Elephants*: "The angle of incidence equals the angle of reflection equals the angle of accidents."

I believe in something like broken ribs.
To know, as far as one can face it,
what happens.

*

Conjurors have prerequisites, according to Henry Dean. These, put forth in Dean's 1772 tome, *The Whole Art of Legerdemain*:

A Description of the Operator.

1. He must be one of a bold and undaunted Resolution, so as to set a good face upon the Matter.
2. He must have strange Terms, and empathetical Words, to grace and adorn his Actions; and the more to amaze and astonish the Beholders.
3. And Lastly, He must use such Gestures of Body, as may take off the Spectators Eyes, from a strict and diligent beholding your Manner of Performance.

The effect, as Dean is alluding to, isn't enough. I was always told, by the guys at the magic shop, by the articles I read in *Genii* and *Magic Magazine*, "The effect isn't good enough – your hands aren't fast enough – until you can fool yourself in the mirror." If you don't jump at the juxtaposition/disappearance/appearance, your audience won't either.

Practice involves two stages: analytic practice – the information is studied; what is the effect, how shall the viewer perceive it, how do I hold the deck of cards, higher, lower, looser, tighter? Next is mechanical practice – the sleight, or movement, is repeated and acquired into motor memory; the movement needs to be an unconscious response to a conscious demand. An illusion is only as good as its practitioner's nervous system allows it to be.

*

The game of *notions*. Tenuous. Anthropomorphic. Sometimes we simply aren't sure of much. Humans have evolved to exert control, to exhibit orientation, but often we are cheated, fooled, misled: purposefully and not. According to Peter Lamont, in his seminal *Magic in Theory: An Introduction to the Theoretical and Psychological Elements of Conjuring*, there are three kinds of Appearance: "object was already there but was concealed," "object was secretly put in position," and "object is not actually there but appears to be." *An apparently impossible case of matter through matter.* An object changes form. Changes places.

Usually cheating, according to Ferric C. Fang and Arturo Casadevall's *Why We Cheat*, occurs where there is competition for limited resources. Scientists have discovered that there are three distinct reasons people cheat: 1) fear of loss, 2) the observation of dishonest behavior by someone else, and 3) creativity. Maybe magicians, then, are simply creative folks who see Nature, politicians, and the uber-wealthy deceiving and want in on the action. Maybe the loss we fear is that we won't be able to maintain control or remain oriented without being manipulative. The difference is we don't manipulate the weather, the Dow Jones, or the Senate.

Fang and Casadevall: "Cheating can breed more of the same if nothing puts a brake on the process. Once someone has overcome the initial barrier to cheating, subsequent hurdles to dishonest behavior may seem smaller and trivial to surmount." Relatedly, cheating, in the human and animal world, is a contagion, is infectious. A magician changes one thing, conceptually, into another. A magician makes an object appear where it was not. A magician makes an object disappear from where it was. And then we do it again and again. For ourselves. For our mirrors. For our camcorders. And finally, for you. Again and again. It's addicting, the high of being in control.

*

I've learned through magic, about empathy (the best magicians, David Copperfield included, especially in his Flying illusion, understand theater and know how to exploit this knowledge of human nature – our wants, needs, and interests), about wonder, about childhood. Children are much more creative than adults. They have not yet lost their capacity for wonder. *They explore,* according to John Carney in his brilliant essay "Secret Philoso-phy," the foreword to Stephen Minch's *John Carney's Carneyco-pia, the most common things with a ruthless curiosity. Ignorant of the consequences, they overcome fear and complacency for the great-er reward of discovery. They don't sit for the rest of their lives; they soon stand up alone and, a step at a time, they learn to walk.*

Being creative – creating magic, creating illusion – is all about making fresh combinations. How can I make this lemon disap-pear and *re*appear over there? How can I make the signed dollar bill I vanished earlier then appear inside the lemon when the spectator cuts it open? We all think differently, we all problem-solve uniquely, and when we apply our uniqueness, we some-times fail, though every time we fail, we get one step closer to the potential solution: *have multiple lemons and only make it* ap-pear *that the ones vanished and reproduced are the same.* The dol-lar bill, however, is the tricky part: *a knife has both a blade and a handle.*

HIATUS: A MEMOIR IN CÆSURA

It's not what you look at that matters, it's what you see.
— THOREAU

I called him Billy. Billy's grandmother called him Nero. I'm not sure of most things about his grandmother's condo, but I do remember the smoke-filled living room, the old man who visited nearly every day to play hand after hand after hand of pinochle and bridge and other card games I still don't understand.

Billy's condo was in the building next to my dad's. McHenry, IL, near the belly of Bull Valley. Dad's building was atop a hill. Go down the hill to the south and face west, you'll see the main intersection into and out of the neighborhood. Turn east, though, and you'll funnel through the complexes and into some single-family homes, pre-fabs, quarter-acre lots, another set of condos, and finally, a park. A baseball diamond, a fishing pond, and a field of eight-foot high reeds, their tips browned-out until late in the summer when the pods flower into a white fluff like cotton candy that billow through the neighborhoods like snow.

*

When I was eight, we dug a hole in our backyard. Backhoes first. Then by hand to create the right depth, the right angles. Finally, post-hole diggers in the corners where we'd anchor the tarps, the ground covers, to flatten the soil beneath the pool's lining. It would be an above-ground pool, but the earth had to be level, had to be deeper still than the land surrounding it–*above* ground. *Below*: it was now a graveyard of stones and petrified soil unearthed for the first time in millennia. And a bone. Oblong, formerly toothed? Oblong, socketed.

The geological strata: the rocks above an unconformity are younger than the rocks beneath, *unless the sequence has been overturned*. Like a dictator, an unruly asshole in a bar: *overturned*. As if lifted, physically, with strength and backbone. An unconformity represents a time during which no sediments were preserved in a region. The local record for that time interval is missing. So the *oblong*? It represented a time, a lull, something once living and dying and now long dead. *The interval of geologic time not represented is called a* hiatus. Perhaps we weren't missing layers of time in the strata of our hollowed yard, but we certainly dug up more than dirt.

The backhoe had swathed and crunched through dirt, rocks, roots. The resulting piles towered over us. *Oblong*: I studied it under the porch light late into the evening. I stole my sister's toothbrush, scrubbed it like I'd seen the curator do at the museum to the fossilized stegosaurus bones. Oblong, pocked. I wanted theory. I wanted answers. A raccoon. That was my stepdad Jim's guess. Too big for a skunk. Too small for a dog. Opossum? I held it against, pressed it to, my skin, opened and closed my mouth, hinged the jawbone–our guess–alongside my own. Felt the way the missing half might have moved in concert.

*

Billy and I spent most of that summer at the park together. On one of those afternoons we made our way to the field of reeds. We kicked at stalks, watched them bob and weave, awed at both their height and their strength. Billy, while not necessarily a mean kid, would sometimes get this look, this glaze over his eyes. It was, I admit, a bit scary, like he was possessed by both great strength and great stupidity simultaneously. Once I saw him stick a spoke through a kid's bike tire as he rolled by *just because*. But he wasn't a bad kid all the time, just a kid who spent the weekends with his chain-smoking relatives ignored and set free into the neighborhood.

I remember telling my dad about *Nero*. We looked it up together: Nero Claudius Caesar Augustus Germanicus was Roman Emperor from 54 to 68, the last in the Julio-Claudian dynasty. After the Great Roman Fire in 64, some Romans believed Nero himself had started it in order to make room for his new palatial estate. Known as the Emperor who "fiddled while Rome burned," he's also known for many executions, including those of his mother and his stepbrother. And lest he had to sit on his terrace in the dark, he was known to capture Christians and burn them in his garden at night for a source of light. I think my dad knew Billy wasn't the greatest influence, but since he and my mom had split and I had to visit his place every other weekend, he seemed pleased enough that I had a friend in the neighborhood.

*

From the other room, as I drifted to sleep and nightmares and dreams, the war began every night at 10:00 PM CST on ABC. And NBC. And CBS. War on Simulcast. Cruise missiles thousands of miles away flashed across our screen. The boom and light when they struck buildings. Reporters praying the building they stood atop wasn't the next target. The rubble. The first reality TV show. Tom Brokaw. Ted Koppel. George H.W. Bush. Figureheads and voices.

The war didn't mean much to me. Its context. Its content. The hows and whys both insignificant and yet omnipresent. But I could see it, watch it, listen to it nightly. Tanks, armored and not, loud and sometimes muted, rumbled over deserts and through towns. The men popped their heads out of the cockpit, waved at the civilians, looked proud and dignified, but the children on the streets clung to their mothers and fathers, and grandparents sat cross-legged on the sandy ground, their eyes pinched, their hands folded knowingly.

*

Forty eighth graders. Six adult chaperones. We scattered throughout the plane, sat with whom we wanted. Each aisle had four seats. I took the third seat, next to a businesswoman I didn't know. I wanted a window seat, but by then they'd all been taken. This was as close as I'd get.

I recognized the rite-of-passage-ness of the the eighth-grade trip to Washington, D.C.

We packed our Sony Discmans, our copies of *Doggystyle*, earbud headphones, and indestructible attitudes: *From the depths of the sea, back to the block / Snoop Doggy Dogg, Funky, yes, but of the Doc.*

The plane taxied, turned left onto the runway, picked up speed, and soon started to rise until the back wheels peeled off the pavement, and we circled to the right, high above O'Hare. I held my breath, squeezed both armrests, chomped my gum.

Out my window, darkness clamped the city shut, but its lights, its lights.

"Sorry," I said to the woman next to me.

*

As Billy and I kicked around in the stalks, something caught my eye in the sunlight. Something metal, something I'd never seen before. A drainage pipe, wide and with serrated edges like a freshly opened can. A weak stream trickled from it. Billy's smile told me all I needed to know: we were going in. He ran in first. No hesitation. Ran full speed, crouched, a bit, to avoid slamming headfirst into the top of the pipe. I soon lost sight of him in the dark. I followed.

The humidity dropped by half about ten feet into the pipe, as if we'd already descended hundreds of vertical feet when in reality we weren't more than a yard beneath the soil. When I couldn't see my hands in front of my face – about twenty or so steps in – I started to turn around, yelled, "Billy!" I didn't hear a response. I didn't hear his footfalls anymore. I didn't hear anything except the echo of birds – or reeds being whistled, through, by the wind – from beyond the opening of the pipe. I was a cautious kid, far too afraid to venture into unfamiliar darkness, but Billy had no fear. I called him again, "Billy!" Nothing. "Nero!" It was as if he'd vanished through time's folds, walked through some kind of portal. He was gone.

I saw sunlight again within half a minute. Initially I thought about walking home as if nothing had happened, but then I figured there must be an exit to the pipe. Maybe Billy had managed to traverse the whole damn thing. I stood puzzled and then heard my name over the tops of the reeds.

*

The year I found the jawbone was the year we studied the Grand Canyon in grade school. We learned of The Great Unconformity: the gap in the rock record between Cambrian times (about 550 million years ago) and the pre-Cambrian (anything earlier). Something disturbed sedimentary possibilities. In the stratigraphic column. *Preservation* was not possible. Because: no rocks were formed. Because rocks were formed but eroded away more rapidly than the deposits directly above or below. Small unconformities are ubiquitous: *every cross-bed surface.*

Every comet. Every asteroid. Every visitor. Here's how much larger, more generous, the world can be.

The Great Unconformity represents 250 to 1200 million years in the Grand Canyon, but the disruption is found everywhere across the globe: it divides rocks with similar, familiar fossils from those with no fossils. John Wesley Powell was the first to observe the Unconformity in the Grand Canyon. 1869. *An exceptional example.* The contact – or lack thereof – between sedimentary strata and crystalline strata. Different origins, structures. *Periods of geologic time sufficiently long enough to raise great mountains and then erode them away.*

Remember: you find what you look for.

*

Out my window there were no bombs, no planes or insurgents or rotting bodies, buildings, mortar, brick, and flesh. Just grass and an oak tree, some cars, streetlights, miles of pavement. Sometimes I'd stay awake to watch the coverage. The unreality of the spectacle only made it that much harder to turn away. Real people died, and we watched them run for their lives. Real people fought, and we watched, ate our popcorn, and decided whether we'd mow the lawn tomorrow or on Sunday before we went for a swim or out to lunch or to take a nap.

*

She smiled. Green eyes, high cheekbones, and perfume that smelled like the ocean or a volcano or melted butter or hot dirt or oh-my-god. Brown hair just past her shoulders. Maybe in her late twenties. I put my sweatshirt over my lap.

"It's a short flight," she said. She took off her jacket, turned toward the window, used the jacket as a blanket to cover her thighs and torso. Her calves remained uncovered.

Twenty minutes later or an hour later or five minutes later or two hours later: she moved her arm, bumped me lightly with her elbow. And again, again. So lightly. Her head rested against her seatback, her eyes closed tightly, too tightly, like she was dreaming or nightmaring, like she was in pain. And then her mouth opened, just a little. She exhaled. So controlled, her lips. I studied her brow, her jawline. Even in the dim, I saw her cheeks redden. The vein in her neck tensed.

I didn't dare move.

Finally she licked her lips long and slow. Twice. Her head never moved. Her eyes never opened. She must have been awake. She wasn't dreaming. And neither was I.

*

Billy was covered in mud, his socks and shoes soaking wet. "I squeezed through! It empties into the pond." I'd never seen anyone more proud of themselves. I knew I'd never follow the pipe all the way to its end for I knew walking into my dad's house covered in mud was not an option, but throughout the rest of that summer I ventured further and further into the drainage pipe now that I knew an end existed, that I couldn't get lost, spent hours squatting there. We quickly figured we needed flashlights and other supplies – bottles of water, Pop-Tarts, duct tape, Band-Aids. We put these things in an old grocery bag and kept them on a shelf cut into the pipe some thirty feet inside its entrance. My hours and days vanished into that pipe, Billy by my side. We told stories, caught the frogs we could find. It was phenomenally Freudian, crawling through that dark pipe we knew nothing about—why did it start where it did? What purpose did it serve? We dove into the darkness swiftly and without thought hoping we'd never need to leave, knowing, in some part of our prepubescent minds, that to go forward, deeper, longer, was the only way we'd find out why we were there to begin with.

*

Hiatus. Unconformities in general tend to reflect long-term changes in the pattern of accumulation of sedimentary or igneous strata. Often, these shifts, these sedimentary singularities are *associated with either global changes is eustatic sea level or the supercontinent cycle.* The cycle. Hiatus. An unconformity is a buried erosional or non-depositional surface separating two rock masses or strata of different ages. *In general, the older layer was exposed to erosion for an interval of time before deposition of the younger.* We call this *angular unconformity.* There's a hiatus, a break, an associational subsiding. A jawbone, a boy in a tunnel with another boy trying to learn about his body and its pleasures, a war fought in visual snippets, a woman fucking herself. Summarization cannot be summarized. A hiatus cannot be echoed.

The colder the room you sleep in, the better the chances are that you'll have a bad dream.

This November then, several dreams, several nightmares. Long-term changes. If dreams can be *read*, who would ever wish to be literate?

I took leather shoelaces from Jim's hiking boots. I took a drillbit. A drill. Went out to the garage, secured the jawbone in a vice. Put on sunglasses—to protect my eyes. One hole where the mandibular muscle—the buccinator—had once locked to the bone, had made chewing more powerful on the push than the release. Threaded the leather through, tied it in a loop, slid it over my head, admired it briefly, and then put it down the collar of my shirt. No one else could see it. I knew then something else entirely, something like calm or a landscape zoomed in upon, hills and valleys taken via the long view, the subsequent subsiding, the tectonic uplift, the history of mountain building. To hold geologic time against my chest. To hold something, anything, from beneath the earth closely, to admire it and admonish it simultaneously, took more imagination than I had, but still that jawbone pressed against me helped me nightmare the possibilities.

ANOTHER ANIMAL: VARIATIONS ON A SCENE,
AND A CODA

At thirteen I told my stepdad, Jim, that I loved him. At fourteen
I told Sandy Stryzalka that I loved her. At fifteen I caught, with
a fishing net, four infant raccoons in my mom's basement, told
myself I knew, then, finally, what love was. But the next day,
after Animal Rescue secured a mesh wire plate to the top of our
chimney – to let the smoke out, to keep the raccoons out – Mr.
Morgan, our ninety-one-year-old neighbor, shoveled his own
driveway.

I offered to help. He said no. I offered again. He said no
again. I know now his insistence wasn't annoyance or stub-
bornness or even pride. It was love for routine, or something
like it. For work, for blood flowing to the extremities and back
to its pump. For body aches, or something like them. He shoveled slowly, meticulously, with patience and a steady rhythm,
up and down the driveway, straight lines, never overlapping or
overstepping the lanes he created.

The best thing about cold-weather snow: it packs, is wet,
heavy, and when you shovel it, the edge you create stands,
shows depth, tells you dramatically where you've been, where
you must go next. When it's warmer, or worse, windy, there's no
depth, no physical memory of where you've already shoveled;
it's disheveled, the process, the snow itself, the way an old man

stands against the white background, his wool cap, earflaps buttoned to the sides, his boots nearly past his knees.

Cold is peaceful. Quiet. The way the heart compensates, keeps blood close. The atria swells and fingers stop working. Everything slows down. Everything sounds louder than it is until you feel your heart beating in your wrists and then exhale.

*

Maybe ten below and wind-chilled. We watched a movie, made a fire. And then. The noise was quiet but persistent, rose barely above *The Silence of the Lambs*. Scratching. Or crying. Or a needing, a kneading, a call to or from or against. Or all noises at once.

My girlfriend, us fifteen, said, "it's coming from the fireplace."

"But the fire's burning."

An anguished squeak now. I muted the movie. We heard what sounded like footfalls from inside the chimney – smoke backed into the house, the smell of burrowing earthworms, petrichor, wet leaves – the biology of falling, and one, two – by this time I'd gotten up, turned off the gas to the fireplace – three, four soot-covered infant raccoons bounced from the brick bench at the base of the fireplace to the basement floor.

"Oh. Those are alive," Sandy said. Her bra hung half-on, half-off, down one sleeve of her t-shirt. Mom ran into the room: "What the hell was that?!"

The raccoons, as if on cue, raced from their shock to my mom's feet, stopped – to gather their wits? think, conceive of their purpose? to shock us once more? – and went down the hallway leading to the garage. My mom let them go, didn't try to stop them. I grabbed Sandy's bra, my handiwork of the last twenty minutes completely undone, fruitless, and stuffed it between the couch cushions, whispered to her: "Just cross your arms."

I ran to block the stairs, assumed the defensive position: feet shoulder-width apart, knees bent, back straight, arms to the side. I looked toward the door to the garage, thought maybe the fishing net, the one Jim, who was at work, used to net catfish and muskies.

The summer before I'd caught a forty-four-inch, nineteen -pound muskie on six pound test, a six-foot rod, and a spinning reel. It was exhilarating, the chance of loss, the opportunity to prove not only that I could hook the fish but bring him into the boat on inferior tackle, tackle meant for smallmouth bass, crappie, maybe walleye. It terrified me to think of losing that fish during the thirty minutes it took to land it, but Jim was there, that very net in his hands, and he scooped the monster out of the lake and plopped it onto the floor of the aluminum dinghy. It flopped prehistoric, gills pulsing. I wanted to lift it above my head in triumph. And I did.

With the net in hand I approached the bastard raccoons from behind, thought I could surprise them. But I was wrong. My efforts only herded them back down the hallway into the main room. They settled in the corner, their darkened bodies, their black eyes blacker. We stared at each other, and then we relaxed, all of us, the raccoons didn't move, my mom and Sandy waited by the door for Animal Rescue, Sandy's arms wrapped tightly across her chest. Everything was still again the way the lake is before a bite. And then the knock on the door.

*

Beach Park, IL. May 1985. King Way's Estates. A spring robin burst into my grandma's trailer, sliced its way through the kitchen, took a left turn down the short hall. The neighbor kids, huddled under the dining room table, kept the green-army-man battle going while the robin took refuge atop the chest against the far wall. I crawled under the chaise kitty-corner the chest, my army set in formation at the only door in and out of the room. Grandma stormed in from the kitchen, trampled my men.

"Where'd it go?" We all pointed to the top of the chest. Under the table, Suzy squealed, scared and unsure of things winged.

Grandma: "Shoo, bird. Shoo." She took off her apron, waved it at the robin. "Shoo."

Mom walked in, and when the screen door banged shut, the robin jumped, swooped toward the floor until air caught its wings and lifted it inches before impact with the ground. The robin circled the room twice, gained speed – Suzy screamed, and the boys did, too – finally conquered the room's dizzying gravity and lack of thermal drafts, and buzzed over Grandma's shoulder and Mom's perm. It flew right into the doorframe and dropped hard to the wood floor, its caramel feet docile against its still breast.

*

I strapped on my waders, the rubber hot against my skin, before stumbling through the parking lot. The added weight on my young body made my feet dance their own dance of confusion and malaise. Our legs bowed under our gear as we crossed the embankment to the river shore. I took a few steps into the water; Jeff, my cousin, stayed nearer shore. The water crashed to the bottom of the dam's spill and spit rainbowed clouds of mist and cool into our faces. We baited our hooks, pushed metal through flesh, stained our fingers with blood, but we were meticulous, sure to leave the tail of the worm off the hook: its wiggling meant to induce a bite. We casted to the bottom of the river. The deep cold made the worms frantic. The tips of our poles bobbed and shifted with the river's current, but we waited for the bend, the quick snap and tug of our line. A bite. Jeff wound and wound his reel, dragged the fish against the current. He could barely hold the pole still. The fish broke the surface. It was a male goatfish, a type of carp. It flopped in the shallow water. We kicked and prodded the big goatfish with our feet.

I reached to unhook him, but was afraid of the sharp-edged spines on his dorsal fin. He could slice me to the bone with one flex of his body, one flip of his boned tail. We cut the line and kicked him toward the water; his eyes scraped against the shore gravel. But he was quiet. His lips fumbled with pre-words and I knew what he was saying: *kick me harder, kick me harder, I know how to swim.*

*

They'd been asleep for over six years when I plucked them from the soil between two twigs I wielded like chopsticks. Their noiselessness, their stillness, their skin crispy and thin like dried maple leaves or a sheet of cheap wrapping paper. I roused the cicadas from their slumber. I lay on my belly, got a closer look, shifted the twigs to one in each hand in an attempt to manipulate the numb insects from the dark of underground.

The red of Kentucky stuck to my sweaty skin and my tongue wagged from my mouth. The ground there held heat differently than it did up north. It clawed at me, had personality, mirth, attention – the heat the dirt, the dirt the heat – and grabbed onto my shirt and my pants and my skin: the magnetic attraction of boys to dirt, of dirt to everything else. One by one I lined up my catch. No wind. Only heat. The cicadas neither moved nor stayed completely still but rather seemed to flinch, spill sideways, as my rapid breath so close to the ground, amazed at what I'd found, gently lifted their bodies.

Louisville, or just east of it, on some old family land, a white house, gray shutters, a well, a stand-alone garage, to visit Jim's father. James G. McCay, Sr. retired to the hills of Kentucky where his kin had farmland. He worked the small farm—a couple pigs, a cow, some chickens, a few rows of sweet corn, sunflowers, tomatoes, and sweet potatoes—until his wife died a few years before my visit. He stayed at the farm instead of moving back north, but the land went to shit and he sold the animals to local land-owners for next to nothing.

Eventually I bored of the cicadas. No matter how much I pushed and prodded them, they wouldn't wake up and buzz overhead—the deep, sawing noise of their wings would exist only in conjecture. Finally I washed my hands and face in a basin of rainwater at the foot of the garage, an old pig trough left over from the farming days. The water turned orange as I delighted in my dirt.

Once clean I lumbered through the garage, my face dusted red again after I dried it with my stained shirt. Some rusted tools; a flat tire, the rim bent and flattened on one side; a push-mower, still shiny and sharpened. And then, in the corner, a rifle, an old one. Dark metal plates screwed meticulously into a marbled brown, almost black, wood. It looked heavy, distinguished, like something of a relic, passed down, treasured as if a family's legacy depended on it. Attached just below the barrel, a bayonet, gleaming, glinting silver. I wanted it. I didn't know what I'd do with it, but I needed it.

I picked it up, marveled at its heft, its potential history. When raised and aimed, the butt caressed in the crease between my cheek and my shoulder, it felt simultaneously cold and hot, invented and collared.

And then I heard a cacophony, a droned beat. I stepped out of the garage. Hot and windblown, a cloud of cicadas approached from the west, booming and buzzing black and white and blue, bug and cloud and sky. I slung the rifle to my shoulder and stood underneath the noise, closed my eyes and mouth, clicked my heels together to stand straighter, and listened at attention.

CODA

A moment now. To reflect. To analyze. To reappropriate a raccoon from a distance. An ambassador from *what it looks like* and *how it flies*. Narrative only takes us far enough – after that is language, and after that is waking.

The ark. Aesop. Bugs Bunny. The holy trinity of animals and their stories. Some kind of wilderness. Something about animals. Our lives. The intertwining of all we love, could love – the scars that survive – a dress made of cicadas. Or everything for clarity's sake. Oil on panel. Gutenberg, or tongue and ears before that. The click of consonants against teeth, the fleshy vowels that ride the guttural ridge, the palette. Canvas. Gopher wood. What isn't clear is clearly in the distance, and what's distant is patient, rectified, the bell-shape of the mouth at holler. Fables exist, and they teach us so much about the purgatory between waking and dreaming.

Butterflies, if hot enough, will land only in the shade, even if it means starvation. The medium is meaningless if hardly anything in the universe is a human being. What I don't know about hibernation. What I don't know about incubation. What I don't know about the mating habits of the tortoise. Porcupine. Platypus. Paca. Peccary. Peacock. Pelican. Pheasant. Plover. Pronghorn. Puma. Palm squirrel. There's music, especially, in what we know but haven't touched. And that's just the hovering of it. The distinction between ideas and desires, history and narrative. Music and image. To be overwhelmed by scale alone is to accept the necessity of story, of how one mouth to one ear and the whole world suddenly was.

From the not-voice another animal lifts into being. The nerve endings of a snail shell: hold it to your ear to hear the ocean. Cochlear. I believe in firmament. I believe in stealing with your eyes. Snails that respire using a lung belong to the group *Pulmonata*. Pulmo: of or relating to the lungs. Nata: to be viscous, to stick, to be concentrated on, to adhere. The viscous lung. To concentrate, to disjunct, through breath. To stick, adhere, but better to be buoyant musically. What are we dependent on after all? Facts. Illusions. Niceties. Perceptions. We must be open to stories without heroes. After all, *vulnerable* means "to wound." We are dependent on precision. Snails can have up to 14,175 teeth. On their tongues. The digestive secretions of Tiger Snails decrease human stomach acidity by 42%, thus calming the development of ulcers. In New Guinea, sea snail shells were once used as currency. This we know and from it, power. Currency. An idea we settle on and can love and tell, retell.

There is value in the fictive, but out of truths come the subtleties of denotation. The snail suggests an idea. *Snail* suggests a feeling. I, however, call upon the literal, the primary signification, the hint, the delusion of the referent. Here I told stories. There I defined meaning. Both times I desired. This, then, is the desire: let everything here be more than everything and still be all. We are the liars of no consequences.

POSTLUDE ON DARKNESS

Nighttime as elegy. Nighttime as constraint. Being in the state of. Nighttime's alter-ego: the Jazz Man. Croon, baby. *Croon*. Darkness after light is universal. Or before. We recognize the world, the jaws, the mandibular arc of daybreak.

*

Imagine living in a city before electricity. Paul Bogard, author of *The End of Night: Searching for Natural Darkness in an Age of Artificial Light*, writes that, "...in 1830 what lights did exist [in New York] were intended only as beacons or guides rather than to illuminate the night." Imagination hadn't yet shortened the night. "The New York street lanterns burning whale oil were in 1761 merely 'yellow specks engulfed by darkness,' and even more than a hundred years later its gas lamps were still 'faint as a row of invalid glow-worms.'"

*

I've never been afraid of the dark. Things that go bump. I have fears, no doubt. Just not *what's-in-the-closet*, what's-that-shadow-on-the-wall, *that sound! what is that noise?* Maybe failure. Or silence. But darkness and silence are two different sides of a very similar coin. Darkness: the lack of visual acuity, the distinct absence of optical cues. For which to maneuver. Silence: hypersensitive visual acuity, but with calmness, without clatter – precision, depth perception. You can hear what you see.

*

the mandibular arc of daybreak...

And its opposite: the sun bowing, dissolving into silhouettes. Sloping. We call this time *twilight*. The gradual gathering of darkness has three stages. Civil: cars need headlights. Nautical: one can navigate via the stars. Astronomical: the faintest stars available in the sector of sky one sees are visible. In other words, *that long blue moment*.

*

I've only been to New York City twice, but one of those times happened to be in the summer of 2010. The Flatiron district. Jim Campbell's installation titled, "Scattered Light." From two A-posts in Madison Square Park, Campbell hung a net of 2,000 LED's that turned on or off when visitors walked by. The result was a set of ghostly, moving silhouettes capable of being seen from hundreds of feet away. I remember walking just closely enough to turn the lights on, then backing off until they switched dark again. Over and over. Really, I just wanted to get to the bookstore, but the scatter, the secret on-and-off, the way I felt, momentarily, crepuscular: my pupils expanded, my irises relaxed. The light flooded in.

*

The same gene that makes your iris makes your frontal lobe, which controls personality.

*

But we expect darkness. We crave it, have for millennia fought our fear of it, waited for its end to hunt, gather. Though in it, through it, we navigated, procreated, birthed. Our ancient core, our *collective*, or *genetic* memories from before we were even human, needs view of the night sky. We are connected to the nuances of our surroundings through their occasional absences; in other words, *nocturnalization*.

*

As the retina ages, its proteins thicken, become, like an old windshield, flaky and cloudy, an accumulation of minuscule chips and dings – *a veiling luminance*. According to Bogard, these proteins "reduce the eye's transparency as they scatter the light coming into the eye." Basically, *contrast*. Surely you've driven at night, on a lonely road, stars visible above the horizon, maybe even the moon's shadow cambered overhead, its playful half-circle etched into the empty passenger seat. Maybe a deer on the roadside. Oh, its eyes: pearly, translucent. Driving at night slows down time, or speeds up time. It depends on how many deer, how many marble-eyes. What I'm really trying to say: a shadow marks arrival and departure, the simultaneity of progression, a slowing down – of time and light and bend: gravity or the unknown arc of space-time. Something of a continuum. And then the speeding up at some burst of light – a flashlight, stroke of lightning, daybreak (even the slow burst of morning is still a burst), headlights – and we're back to seeing shapes unhinged, less shapes, really, and more the things themselves.

LYRICISM OF THE FACT: AN ARCHIVE

Samuel Taylor Coleridge was fond of eating fruit while it was still attached to the tree.

Most of what we smell is accidental.

That damn Weimaraner–barking and pacing–every time someone walks drunk by the house. It's July and I wash my hair at 3:00am to stop the sweating.

The chemical symbol for gold is Au. This comes from the Latin *aurum* which, when translated, means *shining dawn*.

Marriage: what I've done and what I say I haven't done; the line between them is thin as the finest silk sheets.

There was more time between the Stegosaurus and the Tyrannosaurus Rex than between the Tyrannosaurus Rex and you. Stegosaurus lived ~150,000,000 years ago. T. Rex lived ~65,000,000 years ago, practically yesterday comparatively.

Touch cells in the lips make nursing possible; among other things, touch teaches us the difference between *I* and *other*.

Is it true that all creatures love their children? – getting pushed is not falling.

[To wrest love, like a deer roadside unsure whether to run into or out of the woods, from a sleeping body.]

Almonds and pistachios are the only nuts mentioned in the Bible. Salt is mentioned more than thirty times.

Due to time zones, Santa has thirty-one hours in which to do his job on Christmas Eve: about 823 homes per second.

Twenty-nine is the only number that is written with as many strokes as its numerical value.

In Oxford, Ohio, it's illegal for a woman to strip off her clothes in front of a man's picture.

It is bad luck to turn a loaf of bread upside down once a slice has been removed.

[Nostalgia: a thief, a remembrance, what once was and should forever be. I won't let you go.]

NOTES AND WORKS REFERENCED
(in order of appearance)

Some of the facts throughout "Lyricism of the Fact: An Archive" were "found" via @omgFacts and in Noel Botham's *The Amazing Book of Useless Information* (Penguin, 2008).

THE EMPTYING THAT FILLS

Burke, Edmund. *A Philosophical Enquiry into the Origins of the Sublime and Beautiful: And Other Pre-Revolutionary Writings.* David Womersley, editor, Penguin, 1999.

Canetti, Elias. *Crowds and Power.* Translated by Carol Stewart, Farrar, Straus and Giroux, 1984.

Frost, Robert. "Mending Wall." *The Norton Anthology of Modern and Contemporary Poetry*, edited by Richard Ellman, et al, Vol. 1, Norton, 2003, 203–204.

"Nyssa sylvatica." *Wikipedia: The Free Encyclopedia.* Wikimedia Foundation, Inc. June 2010.

Irving, John. *The Hotel New Hampshire.* Ballantine Books, 1997.

Hopkins, Gerard Manley. *Poems and Prose.* Penguin Classics, 1953.

Wright, James. "Autumn Begins in Martins Ferry, Ohio." *The Norton Anthology of Modern and Contemporary Poetry*, edited by Richard Ellman, et al, Vol. 2, Norton, 2003, 416.

Radin, Paul. *The Winnebago Tribe.* University of Nebraska Press, 1970.

Millay, Edna St. Vincent. "Conscientious Objector." *Selected Poems*, Harper Perennial, 1992.

HOW TO COPE WITH RISK

Carson, Anne. *Plainwater: Essays and Poetry.* Vintage, 2000.

Yorke, Thom. "Just." *The Bends.* CD. Capitol Records, 1995.

Wiman, Christian. *My Bright Abyss: Meditation of a Modern Believer.* Farrar, Straus and Giroux, 2014.

Williams, William Carlos. "*From* Asphodel, That Greeny Flower." *The Norton Anthology of Modern and Contemporary Poetry*, edited by Richard Ellman, et al, Vol. 1, Norton, 2003, 311–317.

"Flamingoes." *Wikipedia: The Free Encyclopedia*. Wikimedia Foundation, Inc. June 2014.

Rey, Margaret. *Curious George Feeds the Animals*. Houghton Mifflin Harcourt, 1998.

Rilke, Rainer Maria. *The Selected Poetry of Rainer Maria Rilke*. Translated by Stephen Mitchell, 1982.

WATER HAZARDS AND SAND TRAPS

Cokinos, Christopher. *Bodies, of the Holocene*. Truman State University Press, 2013.

Diamond, Jared. *The Third Chimpanzee: The Evolution and Future of the Human Animal*. Harper Perennial, 2006.

YOUR BODY MOVES THOUGH YOU WISH IT WOULDN'T

Cobain, Kurt. "Pennyroyal Tea." *Nirvana Unplugged*. CD. Geffen Records, 1994.

AN EYE THAT NEVER CLOSES IN SLEEP: A NIGHTBOOK

Millay, Edna St. Vincent. "Dirge without Music." *Selected Poems*, Harper Perennial, 1992.

Pliny the Younger. *Complete Letters*. Oxford University Press, 2009.

Wilde, Oscar. "Lady Windermere's Fan," *The Importance of Being Earnest and Other Plays*. Oxford University Press, 2008.

Canfield, Dr. Ken. *The Heart of a Father: How You Can Become a Dad of Destiny*. Northfield Publishing, 2006.

Canetti, Elias. *Crowds and Power*. Translated by Carol Stewart, Farrar, Straus and Giroux, 1984.

IT'S JUST A BEAR, ASSHOLE

Aristotle. *Nicomachean Ethics*. Hugh Treddenick, editor. Penguin, 2004.

Hugo, Richard. *The Triggering Town: Lectures and Essays on Poetry and Writing*. Norton, 2010.

"...THE INABILITY TO ISOLATE A SENSATION..."

Sobin, Gustaf. "Prelude XI." *Conjunctions*, Issue 43, September 2004, pp. 302.

Hass, Robert. *20th Century Pleasures*. Ecco, 2000.

Rukeyser, Muriel. *The Life of Poetry*. Paris Press, 1996.

Ashbery, John. "My Erotic Double." *As We Know*, Viking Press, 1979.

Horace. *Satires and Epistles*. Oxford University Press, 2011.

Plath, Sylvia. "Morning Song." *The Norton Anthology of Modern and Contemporary Poetry*, edited by Richard Ellman, et al, Vol. 2, Norton, 2003, 598.

ON WHINING

Biss, Eula. "It Is What It Is." *Bending Genre: Essays on Creative Nonfiction*, edited by Margot Singer and Nicole Walker, Bloomsbury, 2013, 195-200.

Greene, Brian. *The Hidden Reality*. Vintage, 2011.

RHYTHM IS ORIGINALLY THE RHYTHM OF THE FEET

Heinrich, Bernd. *Why We Run: A Natural History*. Ecco, 2002.

Bramble, Dennis M. and Daniel E. Lieberman. "Endurance running and the evolution of Homo." *Nature*, 2004, Issue 432: 345.

"Pheidippides." *Wikipedia: The Free Encyclopedia*. Wikimedia Foundation, Inc. June 2014.

Burke, Edmund. *A Philosophical Enquiry into the Origins of the Sublime and Beautiful: And Other Pre-Revolutionary Writings*. David Womersley, editor, Penguin, 1999.

"Milo of Croton." *Wikipedia: The Free Encyclopedia*. Wikimedia Foundation, Inc. June 2014.

BOTH THE BLADE AND THE HANDLE

"Ben Okri." BrainyQuote.com. Xplore Inc, 2016. 15 June 2014.

Jarrett, T.J. *Ain't No Grave*. New Issues Poetry & Prose, 2013.

Lamont, Peter and Richard Wiseman. *Magic in Theory*. University of Hertfordshire Press, 1999.

Steinmeyer, Jim. *Hiding the Elephant: How Magicians Invented the Impossible and Learned to Disappear*. De Capo Press, 2004.

Dean, Henry. *The Whole Art of Legerdemain, Or Hocus Pocus in Perfection*. Walter B. Graham, 1983.

Lamont, Peter. *Magic in Theory: An Introduction to the Theoretical and Psychological Elements of Conjuring.* University of Hertfordshire Press, 1994.

Minch, Stephen. *John Carney's Carneycopia.* L & L Publishing, 1991.

HIATUS: A MEMOIR IN CÆSURA

Thoreau, Henry David. *The Journal of Henry David Thoreau, 1837–1861.* NYRB Classics, 2009.

"Geology." *Wikipedia: The Free Encyclopedia.* Wikimedia Foundation, Inc. June 2014.

POSTLUDE ON DARKNESS

Bogard, Paul. *The End of Night: Searching for Natural Darkness in an Age of Artificial Light.* Back Bay Books, 2014.

Giovanna Sandri, *only fragments found: selected poems, 1969–1998*
Hélène Sanguinetti, *Hence This Cradle*
Janet Sarbanes, *Army of One*
Severo Sarduy, *Beach Birds*
Adriano Spatola, *The Porthole*
————, *Toward Total Poetry*
Carol Treadwell, *Spots and Trouble Spots*
Paul Vangelisti, *Wholly Falsetto with People Dancing*
Paul Vangelisti & Dennis Phillips, *Mapping Stone*
Allyssa Wolf, *Vaudeville*

———————

All of our titles are available from Small Press Distribution.
Order them at www.spdbooks.org